HELP! I'M PREGNANT WITH PURPOSE

Discover, Manifest, and Walk Fearlessly in your
God-Given Purpose Without Delay

Dr. Sherrie Walton

Walton Publishing House
Copyright © 2021 by Sherrie Walton

All rights reserved. In accordance with the U.S. Copyright Act of 1976, the scanning, uploading, and electronic sharing of any part of the book without the permission of the publisher constitute unlawful piracy and theft of the author's intellectual property. If you would like to use material from the book (other than for review purposes), prior written permission must be obtained by contacting the publisher at admin@iamsherriewalton.com. Reviewers may quote brief passages in reviews.

Walton Publishing House
Houston, Texas
www.waltonpublishinghouse.com
Printed in the United States of America

Disclaimer: The advice found within may not be suitable for every individual. This work is purchased with the understanding that neither the author nor the publisher is held responsible for any results. Neither author nor publisher assumes responsibility for errors, omissions, or contrary interpretations of the subject matter herein. Any perceived disparagement of an individual or organization is a misinterpretation.

Brand and product names mentioned are trademarks that belong solely to their respective owners.

Library of Congress Cataloging-in-Publication Data under ISBN: 978-1-953993-08-3, herein.

HELP!
I'M PREGNANT
WITH PURPOSE

Are you ready to discover your purpose and live the life God has for you?

Join Dr. Sherrie on the journey at
www.manifestmypurpose.com

CONTENTS

Dedication .... *vii*

Preface .... *viii*

Introduction *1*

1. Help! Something is Happening 10
2. You are Chosen 26
3. Are You Naked? 41
4. Pregnant with Purpose 57
5. Follow the Path to Purpose 72
6. Identify Your Purpose 90
7. Birthing Purpose 110
8. Your Big Announcement 125
9. Your New Journey 136
10. Live Your Purpose-Full Life 149

Purpose Notes: *161*

Acknowledgments: *164*

About the Author: *165*

Connect with Me! *168*

DEDICATION

THIS BOOK IS DEDICATED to women all around the world that are carrying greatness. My prayer is that through the pages of this book, the Holy Spirit will speak to you, and at the end of our journey together you will birth your purpose.

Dr. Chris, thank you for being an amazing husband and best friend. You have always been my biggest supporter, and I thank God daily that you have been my husband and life partner for over 18 years. You experienced firsthand my process of becoming, and you allowed me the space to evolve without judgment or criticism. Your love and guidance have always been unconditional. *I love you.*

To my children Chris II, Kai-Milan, and Winter: You each bring inspiration and sunshine to my day. You give me the courage and motivation to become the best version of myself. I pray the lessons and principles I have taught you will carry you to the nations of the world. Greatness is in each of you. The world is yours for the taking!

PREFACE

To the women who have failed more than once,
who have questioned why bad things happen to good people,
and have wondered if the dream will ever come true–
this is for you.

After all the hurt, defeat, loss, and trauma –
I want you to know that there is a Promised Land.

Now go and fight those giants and take your stuff!

INTRODUCTION

ONE OF THE MOST frustrating things in life is to wander for years, attempting to discover your purpose. I remember being in that very place some years ago and desperately wanting to find a deeper meaning in my life. It was in that place of feeling hopeless that I started my true life's journey – the discovery of my life's purpose. After my evolution, I began to meet other women who were expe-riencing a similar emptiness who also needed guidance. I submitted to my life's work and founded an organization dedicated to helping women unlock their hidden purpose.

After years of teaching and coaching others, it was finally time for me to write this book and share this proven process with the world. Then it happened! Fear, doubt, and self-sabotage crept in, and I started to fear that maybe there were already too many books written on the topic of purpose. I questioned if what I had to say would be any different or even relevant, and this uncertainty resulted in cluttered mind space and hesitation to move forward. "Purpose is the most searched word on Google, so why tackle this topic and add to the sea of commentaries surrounding it?" I asked myself.

After the battle in my mind, I prayed one last prayer and told God that if this was His will, to give me peace with the decision and a download of wisdom for anyone that would read this book. He graciously did.

As I became passionate about helping others discover their purpose, I promised God that I would continue on this journey, no matter what. By the time we end this journey of discovery together, I am expecting an awakening and fire inside your belly that will ignite you to go forth. As you pursue your purpose, you will realize that there are people assigned to your voice, your message, your product, and your brand. You will discover that there is still room for you, no matter how overly saturated the marketplace may seem. I want this book to be your wake-up call and the push you need to birth your purpose. I want this book to help you understand that you don't have any more time to waste. It's time for you to move forward and walk boldly and instinctively into who you have been created to be.

You may feel like you're not ready, and this is okay as this isn't uncommon when embarking on new territory. I felt the same way when I was first introduced to my life's purpose. However, with each submission of "yes" to God, He helped me pull back the layers and experience my internal rebirthing. I relied on His guidance to heal me and prepare me to take my gift to the world. I did the work required to receive my breakthrough. I learned to dismiss the mind clutter and voices that made me want to stop pushing. I fought and pushed until my physical life began to match with the woman I saw in my dreams. Because of this, I gave birth to my purpose.

Your purpose is your lifeline. Discovering and living in your purpose will be the reason you will want to live and inspire others to live as well. That's why you're here and why you stumbled on this book. As you take this journey with me, I promise not to give you a book full of theories and stories that don't bring you any closer to your purpose or trick you into believing that it's just a simple combination of passion and drive. There is a process to discovering and fulfilling purpose. Our lives are always in motion, and we are constantly learning, growing, and striving to become better, wiser, and more self-aware women. We owe it to ourselves to grow spiritually and mentally and become who God has ordained us to be. We owe it to ourselves to strive to live a life full of purpose.

Your purpose is much deeper than how you feel; it's who you are. It's the essence of your being, and it's the reason God made you. But what does purpose really mean to us, and how does finding it affect our lives? And if so many people are looking for it, why do so few people seem to find it? What does it mean to be pregnant with purpose? These are all good questions. I believe being pregnant with purpose simply means that you are in the process of manifesting a life that solidifies why you are here on this earth. It means that you are ready to walk in that purpose boldly and unapologetically and that you are prepared to leave an imprint on this world, whether big or small. It means that you realize you have a role in serving to manifest God's Kingdom – a place of love and peace.

When it comes to the discipline of purpose, there are three different groups of people:

- Those who fearlessly pursue their dreams.
- Those who give up the fight and settle for life the way it is.
- Those who sit with a bag of popcorn watching, judging, and commenting on the lives of others and never moving forward.

This book was written for the first group. The ladies ready to kick down doors, smash in the glass ceilings and take what rightfully belongs to them. For far too long, we have sat back and watched the enemy raise havoc in our lives while accepting whatever life throws at us without demanding that it offer us better. But after reading this book, I want you to scream out, "No more, it stops here!"

Whether we are friends or strangers, I feel like I am connected to you. I feel like I know you. I know that you're ready to receive and walk in your breakthrough. I also know that frequently you find yourself banging your head against the wall as you try to figure it all out. You and I have connected for this season, this reason, and this purpose – to help you receive the release you deserve. Today is your 'appointed day.'

Are you ready to give birth to purpose? Are you ready to become the powerful woman of purpose you've seen in your dreams? If you've answered "yes," allow me to help you reach your unlimited potential and help you discover your true calling. With the concepts mentioned throughout this book, you will understand who you are and what you are carrying. You will learn how to push out your purpose, nourish and care for it. Giving birth to purpose is parallel to natural childbirth. If you have given birth before then, you may have an idea of what I mean. If you have never given birth before, you need not worry. The explanations throughout the book will be straightforward for you to apply and understand.

God is going to speak to you through the pages of this book and stir up the gifts He has placed on the inside of you. Not only will your gifts come alive, but you will also receive a revelation as you have never experienced before. As I write these words, my stomach flutters as if a thousand butterflies are flying around inside. As you continue to read and my ministry comes alive, you will indeed find, discover, and relate to the seed traits your Heavenly Father has placed inside of you. You will unlock the hidden treasures within.

For the past seven years, I have been on a journey to help women live their best life. It has been an honor to impact thousands of women and inspire them to discover their purpose and unlock their gifts. It is my prayer that you are reading this book because you are ready to push and activate your greatness. When you commit to fulfilling your purpose, you will commit to doing whatever is necessary to see it manifest. I pray with all my heart that this book blesses you and encourages you to live your best life in Christ. I pray that it stirs up your purpose and enables you to run with vigor and hope, with the understanding that God is holding you close and the angels are cheering you on to the finish line. I am passing the baton to you, and after you finish reading this book, I want you to pass the baton on to the next person. I have set the bar and expectations high for this message and the people that it will reach and impact. I declare that my words will leave a legacy on the earth and become so contagious that it ignites the fire in every person who picks up a copy. Yes, I am a big dreamer, but truthfully, I know how the right environment will help you birth your purpose as I have experienced this repeatedly. I also know that when we place a demand on the purpose within by aligning it with the Word of God, we will experience life – an abundant life.

Lastly, I want to encourage you and tell you that your dream has not died. There are so many gifts and talents inside of you, and it's time for you to release them. As your 'purpose midwife,' I am cheering for you and encouraging you to push. It's time for you to get moving!

Father God, I ask that you bless the reader of this book. I ask that their eyes be enlightened to receive everything you have for them. I prophesy to every dead and broken place in their life, and I declare healing, restoration, and the redeeming of their time, self-worth, and opportunities. I declare that she will rise like an eagle in power, strength, and experience Your love. I declare her purpose is being revealed in the earth, in Jesus' Name. Amen!

The Parable of the Talents

"For it will be like a man going on a journey, who called his servants and entrusted to them his property. To one he gave five talents, to another two, to another one, to each according to his ability. Then he went away. He who had received the five talents went at once and traded with them, and he made five talents more. So also he who had the two talents made two talents more. But he who had received the one talent went and dug in the ground and hid his master's money. Now after a long time, the master of those servants came and settled accounts with them. And he who had received the five talents came forward, bringing five talents more, saying, 'Master, you delivered to me five talents; here, I have made five talents more.' His master said to him, 'Well done, good and faithful servant. You have been faithful over a little; I will set you over much. Enter into the joy of your master.' And he also who had the two talents came forward, saying, 'Master, you delivered to me two talents; here, I have made two talents more.' His master said to him, 'Well done, good and faithful servant. You have been faithful over a little; I will set you over much. Enter into the joy of your master.' He also who had received the one talent came forward, saying, 'Master, I knew you to be a hard man, reaping where you did not sow, and gathering where you scattered no seed, so I was afraid, and I went and hid your talent in the ground. Here, you have what is yours.' But his master answered him, 'You wicked and slothful servant! You knew that I reap where I have not sown and gather where I scattered no seed? Then you ought to have invested my money with the bankers, and at my coming, I should have received what was my own with interest. So take the talent from him and give it to him who has the ten talents. For to everyone who has will more be given, and he will have an abundance. But from the one who has not, even what he has will be taken away."

Matthew 25:14-29, ESV

Chapter 1

HELP! SOMETHING IS HAPPENING

> *"The Greatest Tragedy in Life is Not Death, But a Life Without a Purpose."* –Dr. Myles Munroe

THE PHONE BUZZED ON the dining room table and 'Mom' popped up on my screen.

"Hey Mom, how are you?" I asked.

"Motherdear, went home to be with the Lord," she responded with a slight shakiness in her voice. My heart immediately sank as I stared blankly while everything around me suddenly became a blur.

Have you ever felt as if your entire world was spinning out of control? As if everything that you had meticulously organized and carefully planned had at a moment's notice taken a deep dive? That explains how I felt the day I received that unexpected call from my mother.

'Okay, I'll call you back. Please keep me updated on the funeral arrangements', and with that, we hung up the phone. I sat there for a little bit and began to reminisce about how both of my parents were burying their mothers just a few months apart. I also remembered my husband's words when he encouraged me to say goodbye to my grandmother a month earlier as we were visiting my parents because he felt she wouldn't survive her illness. I am so happy that I listened to him. But even saying goodbye to her that final time did not prepare me for the reality that she had passed away.

Dealing with her death as her self-proclaimed favorite grandchild was just one of the things that tugged at me in May of 2016. Two years before her death, I had committed to God that I would walk fully into the call on my life. I made a vow to Him that I would stop running from ministry and helping others in the manner that I was supposed to. I made a verbal agreement that I would go – even if I had to go alone. I was afraid, but I was also tired of figuring things out on my own, and I was tired of running. Do you know that feeling of submission that comes as a result of exhaustion? It's a combination of emptiness, hopelessness, frustration, and confusion, all bundled into one. If you know anything about Jonah, then you can probably visualize what it's like to run from God when you have a mandate on your life. *I ran, and I ran* until finally there was no other choice but to throw my hands up and surrender. I would love to say that I willfully submitted – but that just wouldn't be the truth. My 'come to Jesus' moment sounded something like this, *'Well, God, I guess you aren't giving me a choice, so here I am.'* When God wants to get my attention, He will remove the people I feel are necessary for my life and shut the doors of what I believe are opportunities to lead me in the right direction. Can you relate to what I am talking about?

In November 2015, I was led to create and organize the Mommy and Me Dream Bigger Tour, and its second stop was scheduled for Dallas, Texas on May 14, 2016. I had been planning the conference for months; it was my first time hosting an event out of my own city. So many things had transpired for me from the first event in January, including planning the event solo, making my own connections in a new city, and doing it without any big-name sponsors or backing. I am thankful that God surrounded me with dedicated women that believed in me and the vision, and despite the things that were going wrong, they stood by my side as I ventured into unchartered territory. My biggest supporter and anchor was my husband Christopher, and although he was running everything behind the scenes, he was the rock that held me up during one of the most challenging times of my life. He saw the vulnerable Sherrie that often questioned if I was good enough as I discovered who I was in that new space. The speaker's circuit wasn't the most welcoming as I often encountered women who expressed my resume wasn't impressive enough to hold a room, let alone host a conference. *(Thank God, they weren't the ones that called or anointed me).* Chris reassured me daily that despite how things appeared, I would come out on top, and I desperately hoped that he was right. I leaned in on his faith when mine became weak.

When my mother called to discuss the funeral plans, she informed me that my grandmother's funeral would be on May 14, 2016, which was the same day as my 'Mommy and Me' event. The funeral would be held in Miami while I was scheduled to be in Dallas. *Okay God…we have a problem. Do you want me to cancel the event and attend the funeral? I can't do both.* So many conflicting thoughts raced through my mind causing me to retreat to my Prayer Closet to pray. My Prayer Closet has been my safe place for years and the place where God speaks to me. That day in the closet was dreadful. I had a long and heavy talk with God while I was sitting there as words of comfort, direction, and healing were so needed at that time. I am in no way comparing myself to Jesus Christ, but I received a little glimpse of His experience while He was in the Garden of Gethsemane. I remembered putting on my headphones and listening to the song 'Oceans' by Hillsong as tears rolled down my face.

"God, what are you saying to me?" I asked as I cried.

"You are in the middle of giving birth, and you must push. There will always be a reason for you to stop and turn back, but if you stop now, you will abort your purpose." He answered.

Wait! What's happening? There were things that I understood about what was going on, but there were many things that were a blur. Up until that time, I hadn't fully experienced the pain of birthing purpose, although I was familiar with making bold moves. Two years before that day, my family relocated to Houston, leaving everything and everyone familiar behind. Years before that, I left my cushiony job in Corporate America to pursue my business full-time, but as bold as those moves were, this pain felt different. Those were labor pains; this was the actual birthing process.

Why was I facing one of the most challenging decisions of my life after I had surrendered everything to God? Was I being punished? The direction I received went against what my heart was telling me to do.

I questioned if God would put something so difficult on my shoulders that would challenge everything I knew about loyalty and family? Would He tell me to choose the opposite path of what I felt was the right thing to do?

I had so many questions for God, but that didn't change the fact that I had a decision to make, and I had less than two weeks to do it. I spoke with my husband about it, and he held me as I cried on his chest. He knew how difficult it was for me. I proceeded with planning the event and decided to stretch my faith and step out on the water. Okay, this is the part of the story where everything perfectly came together, and Heaven opened while the dove descended. Well, not exactly.

Actually, it was the total opposite. Just as I decided to proceed with the event, more storms began to arise. The first obstacle was the tickets weren't selling as quickly as anticipated. To make matters worse, the promised sponsorship dollars were reduced at the last minute, which affected the budget target. *Houston, we have a problem. Surely I must be doing something wrong.* After reading this, you may be asking, "What did you do?" I did what any desperate believer would do. I called a fast and prayed with my team. If I could have done a rain dance, I probably would have done that too. 'Keep walking Sherrie,' I said to myself.

When the day finally arrived, I watched as God moved me out of the way as I submitted the event to Him. I stood in front of over a hundred plus attendees and vulnerably shared with them that my grandmother was being celebrated in her homegoing service while I wasn't there with my family because I chose to be obedient to my assignment. I attempted to hold back the tears as the pain was great, and somehow I knew if I continued on the path, it would all make sense. That day I witnessed the transformation of the lives of many women, and the testimonies that emerged offered me the reassurance I needed to understand my sacrifice was not in vain. I gave birth to purpose and helped impact the lives of women. Obedience and submission to my assignment birthed the breakthrough in someone else's life. I won't say the process was easy because that wouldn't be the truth. It didn't feel good to me while I was experiencing the birthing process, but I understood the why after I witnessed the results.

I shared that very personal story with you because we often admire people standing on stages around the world, and we celebrate their results, but rarely do we know their process and their pain. I want to prepare you for the process and pain of giving birth to your purpose. I am convinced the process is the reason why many people stop halfway through and retreat. They lose sight of the promise, and they focus only on the pain. I learned some unbelievably valuable lessons about purpose after that event that I want to share with you.

In the birthing room of purpose, you'll discover:

- Your purpose is your light. It's the pre-destination of your life designed to bring help, healing, and clarity to yourself and others.

- Life doesn't miraculously fall in place because you decide to pursue your purpose. Purpose requires more than a decision; it takes action.

- The most difficult decision you will make will be to pursue your purpose. It will require a willingness to sacrifice everything you have become comfortable with.

- The more significant the impact, the bigger the obstacles you will encounter.

- The birthing of purpose will be a spirit-led act, and it's nothing you can manifest relying on your human strength alone.

- What you taste, touch, feel, and see will be different from what you birth.

- The process is painful. However, the results are worth it.

- When you submit to the process, each level becomes easier to endure.

> *"Don't wish it was easier; wish you were better.*
> *Don't wish for less problems; wish for more skills.*
> *Don't wish for less challenge;*
> *wish for more wisdom."*
> Jim Rohn, Motivational Speaker

What is Purpose?

According to the Oxford dictionary, purpose is defined as 'the reason for which something is done or created or for which something exists.' I define purpose as the very existence of who you are, the reason that you have been put on this earth. It's your why. Purpose is the breath that God breathed into you when He gave you life. Purpose is your superpower. It is the thing that sets you apart from anyone else, your identity and unique blueprint, your calling, and your anointing. Purpose is the fabric of your DNA; it is your birthright. Purpose is your wealth and legacy. Purpose is your voice and your connection to others in this world.

Purpose is your gift. Purpose is your strength. Purpose is impactful!

Awakening of Purpose

Purpose identified is the ability to manifest your inner gifts, unique personality, strengths, wisdom, and insight to positively and productively impact and inspire others' lives. Pursuing your purpose will teach you many things about yourself, but it will teach you even more about God. When you take the time to know God more intimately, He will reveal everything about who you are to you. He wants you to know who you were created to be. This shouldn't be a mystery. Discovering and walking in your purpose is just as important as breathing. Fulfilling your purpose gives your life meaning and motivates you to grow, live, evolve, and become an unstoppable force.

The opposite of this is aimlessly moving about just trying to find your way. This aimlessness appears in many forms. It's working a job you hate or being in a relationship that drains you and no longer serves who you are. It's picking a particular career because it seems to be the only option available to you. It's hoping and wishing that you happen to bump into a happiness that is neatly groomed and dressed in a sharp suit. Living your life like this will bring you unfulfillment and a lifetime of restlessness, bitterness, and frustration. But I am sure you know this already – that's why you're here.

Are you beginning to sense an awakening taking place in your spirit? The awakening may be showing up in one of these different forms. Maybe you are starting to have dreams about your life. Perhaps you are spending countless hours researching on the internet and reading about a topic. Perhaps you have discovered that thing that you've become so immersed in that you can do it for hours without realizing it. Or maybe you keep running into strangers that ask you if you are in a particular profession or calling. Perhaps you keep noticing a recurring problem in others, and you know you have the solution. All of these scenarios are clues that God is sending your way to get your attention and cause you to question yourself, where you are right now, and to help you discover your purpose.

These soul-searching moments are the environments for the incubation and birthing of purpose. The more you start to inquire, the more you will discover that the answers are inside you and in the Word of God. The answers are also in others that have been assigned to you to help you birth purpose. It's this shift that has drawn you to this book. You have dreams that you want to see fulfilled, and you know that it's your birthright to have the promises manifested in this lifetime. You have been feeling uncomfortable and uneasy with your life and some of your life choices. The more uneasy you feel, the more restless you become.

You also know that who you want to be will require you to level up. You'll have to get rid of the old thoughts, habits, and undisciplined ways. You'll have to release some relationships and say goodbye to some friends and family. Yes, something is happening; I call it the 'Awakening of Purpose.' It's the feeling you haven't quite been able to identify, but it's caused you to question if there is more to your life. It's the tingling you feel when you listen to people who give motivational speeches that fire you up and cause you to wonder – what if? What if you went for it? What if you stepped out on faith? What if you stopped making excuses and tapped into your potential – what if?

One of my favorite sayings throughout my life has been, "when the teacher is ready, the student will appear." One day the Holy Spirit corrected me and said, "When you seek you will find, when you knock the door will be opened to you." (Matthew 7:7). The next verse states that "For everyone who asks receives, and he who seeks finds, and to him who knocks it will be opened." This means that as long as you keep looking for your purpose, you will discover it.

As a true believer in transparency, I must tell you that purpose typically doesn't show up in your life solely because you want it to or because you expect it. In fact, it will probably show up at the most inopportune time when you least expect it. I shared my story with you about missing my grandmother's funeral earlier to let you know how difficult it can be to walk the unbeaten path and also show you there is victory on the other side.

When you are pregnant with your purpose, you feel different. Like a baby in a mother's womb, purpose does not just go away. It grows inside of you until your body is ready to push. In a natural pregnancy, there is a preparation that must take place before you give birth. This is the same in the supernatural. As you move towards your purpose, you will encounter limiting beliefs and distractions that will attempt to delay you. Don't allow them to overshadow who you have been called to be. Be bold in your decision to move forward and avoid the Anti-Purpose Cycle.©

The Anti-Purpose Cycle©

While stepping out in faith, I realized more than ever what I was called to do. When I accepted my purpose, women from all over the world started to connect with me. They were primarily professional women that had successfully climbed the corporate ladder and proudly displayed the word 'Boss' on their chest. On the outside, these women were the epitome of style and grace. Their hair was in place, their nails neatly manicured, and their wardrobe appeared as if they had stepped out of a Vogue fashion magazine. To the naked eye, they appeared as if they had it all together. They were amazing, powerful, and strong. Anyone looking at them would have wanted to be in their shoes. They had achieved great careers, had plenty of money in the bank, and often a man hanging onto their arms. They said and did all the right things in public, posting motivational quotes, quoting scriptures, and serving their community. They had multiple degrees and social influence to show they were on top of the world. But even with everything seemingly going well for them, something was missing.

When I questioned whether they were living their life with purpose, like clockwork, they would admit they weren't. It's not because they didn't want to, and it's not because they lacked confidence, and even more surprising was the fact that it wasn't fear that was keeping them stuck. It was the busyness of life that kept them from sitting still long enough to hear directions from God. It was their inability to say "no" when someone called to ask them for their advice or if they would help oversee a new committee. They would go on and on about how they were too busy to look after themselves; their careers were demanding, and managing their children's lives consumed them. With so many extra-curricular activities like homework and preparing dinner, there was hardly any time left for them to think about themselves. If they were married or in a committed relationship, involved in their church, or working a side hustle, the amount of free time was even more scarce. I became exhausted just listening to how hectic their schedules were – it frequently changed, sometimes hourly. The demands left little time for them to spend time alone focusing on themselves. It wasn't their fault, but somehow, they became caught up in the cycle.

There was a problem, and I knew that I had the solution. I did not doubt these women were busy, and they loved their families and valued their careers, but they were giving more to others and cutting themselves short in the process. During our conversations, I challenged them to envision a life where they felt fulfilled and motivated and took part in activities that led them closer to their purpose. I challenged them to see themselves living the life that God had designed for them instead of living the life they had meticulously crafted for themselves. One by one, the lightbulbs started to come on.

They started taking their lives and their dreams back. They started holding themselves accountable to living a life of purpose, even if it meant taking a pay cut or cutting back on activities that were tiring them out. I challenged them to build their spiritual walk, let go of the wheel, and allow God to direct their lives for them. I challenged them to give birth to their purpose.

I am not in any way insinuating this is an easy thing to do. We can all be guilty of living in the Anti-Purpose Cycle©. I am not exempt; I constantly remind myself not to get caught up in this cycle. Our world's system, orchestrated by Satan, is designed to keep us stuck there. He knows that true revelation of purpose will only happen when you sit still. God doesn't speak in chaos; He speaks in the stillness of life. He doesn't force you to sit and commune with Him. He's a gentleman. A good life includes serving others, but it also includes refueling and getting appropriate rest. It includes relying on God as the source of provision and not just college degrees and networks. It includes enjoying life instead of allowing the years to pass by without fulfilling your true calling. **It includes living and operating in your purpose.** I encourage you to break free from the Anti-Purpose Cycle©.

If you're honest, you can admit that it leaves you feeling empty and unfulfilled. I challenge you to push past this cycle. I have seen the cycle play out one too many times and it doesn't end well. It looks like this: career, care for others, busy activities, exhaustion, repeat. The Anti-Purpose Cycle©

doesn't stop until you stop it. But that's why you're reading this book, right? It's time for you to walk in your purpose.

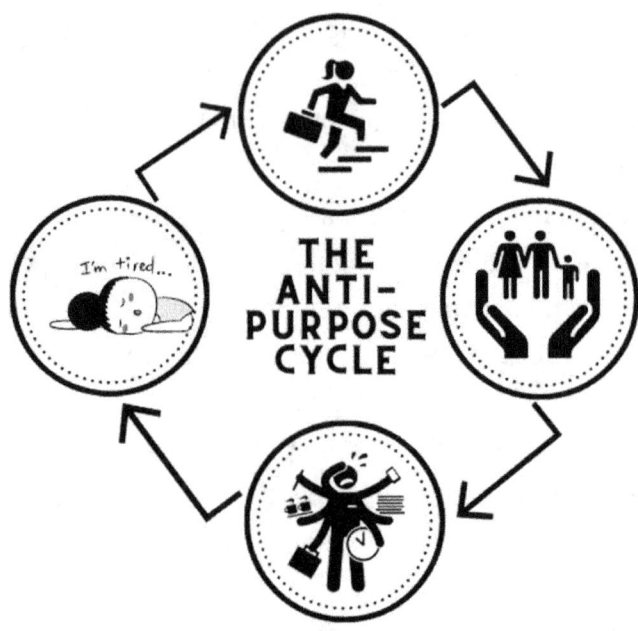

Make a decision and commitment from this day forward that you will not allow anyone or anything to stand in the way of you fulfilling your purpose – including yourself. There is so much greater that God has for you, but it will require you to do things differently than you've been doing them. It's time for you to submit your life, your schedule, and life commitments over to God and allow Him an opportunity to reconstruct you. It's time for you to let Him have complete control. It's time for you to give birth to your purpose.

Chapter I: Recap

- The hardest decision you will make will be to pursue your purpose.

- The process is painful. However, the results are worth it.

- Purpose typically doesn't show up in your life only because you want it or expect it. In fact, it will probably show up at the most inopportune time when you least expect it.

- Fulfilling your purpose gives your life meaning and motivates you to grow, live, evolve, and become an unstoppable force.

- Your soul-searching moments are the environments for the incubation and birthing of purpose.

Chapter II

YOU ARE CHOSEN

> *The Lord turned to him and said, "Go in the strength you have and save Israel out of Midian's hand. Am I not sending you?" "Pardon me, my lord," Gideon replied, "but how can I save Israel? My clan is the weakest in Manasseh, and I am the least in my family." – Judges 6: 14-15*

As you prepare to give birth to your purpose, I want you to acknowledge how amazing and significant you are to your Heavenly Father. It will be difficult for you to accept your purpose until you first learn to accept that you are a part of God's original plan. Life has a way of pushing us around, and if we are not careful, we can become jaded and cynical and see ourselves as less than qualified for our assignment. You are chosen and qualified to fulfill your purpose. In fact, God chose you before the foundation of the world, and no matter what you have experienced up until this point, it doesn't change the fact that you are chosen. Your birth was not an accident. Despite how you arrived or the vessel used to birth you, everything about you was purposely orchestrated and fashioned for you.

The significance of the day you were born not only changed history, but it signified a miracle performed by God in the earth realm. It doesn't matter if your entrance into this world was heralded by a special fanfare by your parents, grandparents, and loved ones, or if it entailed the silent embarrassment of a teenage mother giving birth in a cold lonely hospital room. It doesn't matter at all because it was special to God.

When you accept this truth and walk boldly and unapologetically in it, you'll remove the pressure to receive validation from others. Please allow me to stay here for a bit with you because I don't think we spend enough time celebrating ourselves. As women, we often spend so much time making a fuss over everyone else, and we downplay ourselves to the point that many of us don't even celebrate our birthdays. We are often stuck in the recurring cycles that scream to us that we are not enough or don't matter. Nothing you can do can remove the value of who you are. It's often challenging to see life from this lens, especially when everything you see is telling you otherwise. The world asks us to prove our worth, while our Heavenly Father just wants us to be. It's that simple.

Who Me?

I can vividly remember the Sunday my family joined our new church. I was just 15 years old at the time. A few months before joining as a family, my parents would drive me to the church's youth ministry that gathered on Friday nights. It was an entirely new experience as I observed the youth praising and worshipping God and preaching from the Bible. It was amazing. Before then, I had never experienced teenagers committed to serving God because they wanted to and not just because their parents forced them. The weekly youth sessions were impactful in my life, and after a few short months, I was starting to have a better understanding that God could use me at an early age. I wanted to get to know Jesus Christ the way those other youth knew Him.

I accepted Jesus into my life at the early age of six years old. I don't remember all of the details, but I knew it was something special by the reaction I received from my mom and the other church mothers. The smiling, applauding, and praising God while the pastor led me into prayer was an indication that I was doing something pretty important. Being so young, I don't remember having a personal experience with God. I attended church like most religious people did – going through the motions while my parents instilled in me Christian foundations at home. I was young and wasn't really into a godly lifestyle; however, since I was a minister's kid, it was a requirement that we attend multiple

Sunday services: Bible study, Youth ministry, and any special occasion in between. I guess you could say I was at church quite a bit.

That particular Sunday, we approached the altar at our new church as a family, all seven of us. We huddled close as the pastor asked the congregation to join in celebrating the new believers coming to accept Christ. There were also people gathered at the altar, deciding to recommit their lives to Christ. Others wanted to receive the baptism of the Holy Spirit with the evidence of speaking in tongues. Some wanted to join the congregation. We were there for the latter. The pastor began praying and touching each individual as my parents, my younger siblings, and I stood there as we waited for him to touch us. With a swift movement, he abruptly stopped in front of me.

"Whose child is this?"

I stood there frozen.

Had I done something wrong?

Did he see me smiling at the boy at the back of the church?

Did he catch me writing and not paying attention as he preached his sermon?

I looked back at my parents.

"She's our daughter," they both responded. *Whew, thankfully they claimed me!*

"The favor of God is all over this child. God has marked her," the pastor said with strong conviction. I am not sure if he said much more, but after that, everything else was a blur. I was puzzled, and I wondered what he was talking about. I hadn't heard much about favor before, and I didn't know how profound that pronouncement was back then.

The ushers whisked us away to a room with the greeters, and I can't remember if my family and I ever discussed that 'special favor' again. In fact, I completely forgot about the Prophetic word until favor started showing up in my life some years later – opening doors I knew by man's standards that I wasn't qualified to walk through. That anointing caused me to rise in the workplace from being a temporary front-desk Administrative Assistant to an Insurance Broker with an office and a view and being mentored by one of the top Insurance Brokers in a Fortune 500 company. I can admit that only God could have given me that opportunity.

Although that declaration was made over twenty-five years ago, I still recognize even today how it manifests in my daily conversations. I have spoken with countless strangers who mention they are unsure why they answered my call or responded to my out-of-the-blue email. They are drawn to me, and they don't know why. They may not know why, but I do. I used to take this gift for granted, and truthfully, I didn't even realize that it was an actual gift. But I don't take it for granted anymore.

When you walk through your discovery of purpose in chapter 5 of this book, you will identify and unwrap those gifts that have left clues in your life. It is usually the things that we do easily or work out in our favor with little effort that gives us hints about our purpose. We can often get so caught up in doing that we don't take a moment to ask the question, "why?" Why did you get the position that everyone else was turned down for? Why did you get approved for the loan when the odds were stacked against you? Why did you get pregnant when so many other women tried and couldn't? Why did you beat cancer or survive the car accident? Why you? I'll tell you why. Because everything that has happened to you so far, every door (closed or open), every failure, every success has been leading you to your purpose—even the things you regret.

Discovering my purpose helped me better understand why God created me the way He did. While not always seen as a gift throughout my younger years, my strong-willed personality makes sense to me now that I am living in my purpose. The gifts – small, great, and even seemingly insignificant constantly led me to my purpose and allowed me to connect with the people that need what I have, people who I wouldn't have naturally known. Understanding who I am – who God created me to be – gives me a boost of confidence when I walk through the open doors that would have normally been closed to me. It also keeps me humble because I realize I could never open those doors or make the connections I need based on my own merit.

During that church service over twenty-five years ago, God announced that He had chosen me. However, that wasn't the first time He told the world about me. My first announcement, like yours, was my birth. You see, even if my pastor hadn't called me out that day, God had already called me. The mere fact that I am breathing and living indicates there is more work for me to do. The same applies to you. The fact that you beat out the other potentials in your mother's womb says a lot about you as well.

So maybe you are thinking, your story seems very "motivational like" Sherrie. But, I didn't have a pastor tell me there was a special call on my life, and often I am still trying to discover who I am. Do me a favor and keep reading. I have something for you. You may not have received a grand announcement from man or a declaration like Jesus received when He was baptized by John the Baptist, and the Heaven opened, and the dove descended on His shoulder with a loud voice reaffirming Him. How loud your announcement is or isn't does not change how valuable you are to your Father. You are carrying something valuable that He placed on the inside of you.

A Beautiful Soul

I had the pleasure of working with a client in China who shared with me the tragedy surrounding her birth. Her name is Tracy, and she was born and raised in Zimbabwe. Her mother was hired as a prostitute and raped by her father. He later disowned both her and her mother as he went back home with his family. Out of that union was born a beautiful soul. Contrary to what anyone would tell her, she was not an accident.

My heart went out as I heard the pain in her voice as she told me her story. For over thirty years, she dealt with the spirit of shame. As the Holy Spirit gave me the words, I began to speak life into her and her purpose. After one session together, she told me that no one had ever spoken to her like that or had helped her find her voice. After a few sessions with me, she was smiling, feeling free, and had rediscovered the little girl buried so deep underneath the layers of pain. She broke the shame of her past that she had carried as a heavy weight most of her life. The spirit of shame affected every area of her life, and the enemy used it to paint her darkest days. When our sessions ended, she wrote a book, and she began to grow her non-profit business. Her freedom is nothing that I can take the credit for; I simply told her what God said about her, and she believed it. It was that simple. When she wrote me the following testimonial, I was overwhelmed with joy.

"I would like to thank God for Dr. Sherrie Walton. The first time I spoke to her in China, we talked for more than an hour. I was overwhelmed with life's challenges. She encouraged me to write the book telling my life experience. By then, I was just saying to myself, does Dr. Sherrie know that I don't even have a computer to write the story? I had given up on life. My heart was tired, and I felt like I could not take it anymore. With her words of encouragement, I can face my today with confidence.

Later on, I told her my story of shame and that I was always crying for more than 38 years. My heart was full of unforgiveness. I was bitter with my father for abandoning me when I was young. I was bitter with everything around my world. I was bitter with friends, workmates, and the way I was raised. Every time I wanted to explain something, I would cry and I would feel like I had a strong wound bleeding in my heart.

That wound caused me to shed tears. Even the time I spoke to Dr. Sherrie, I was crying so badly. She kept telling me that I was not defined by my past experiences. I would like to thank God, who mightily used her to change my life. She gave me scriptures that penetrated through my heart and healed the wounds. My life moved from the place of Satanic bondage to a place of Godly freedom. I am now living a free life. I am out of self-pity, bitterness, hate, and unforgiveness. Dr. Sherrie, may the Lord help you to continue doing His work transforming the lives of many women in the world."

A few months back, I checked in with Tracy. She told me that her non-profit earned enough money through its T-shirt sales to send thousands of surgical masks to the hospitals in Zimbabwe. I smiled with tears in my eyes as she bragged about how she was able to move forward in her purpose. After our call, I began to thank God for the opportunity to serve more people. Tracy didn't know that one of my goals and prayers is to touch the lives of a million people around the world. I don't know how I'll do it, and that's not my responsibility to know the specifics. My only focus is to walk in my purpose and let God do the rest. Not only was I able to help Tracy, but through her, I also helped people in Zimbabwe. What I am saying is the gift of purpose is one that keeps on giving and multiplying.

God Can Use a Broken Vessel

Tracy is just one of the many testimonies that I can share about how my obedience to purpose unlocked someone else's purpose. I know it has nothing to do with me. I remember walking in shame and condemnation due to the choices I had made in my life. I struggled for a long time with how God could use someone like me. I was a liar, a cheater, and a manipulator, and had God not stopped me in my tracks, there is no telling where I would have ended up. I hurt people in the process and shattered the trust of some people that trusted me; often, those closest to me were the most affected. I pushed the envelope far too many times, and by the grace of God and only because of His mercy, I was able to be delivered and set free from myself. There were character flaws that needed to be dealt with, areas that I needed to mature in, and bridges that I had to mend.

Graciously, He allowed me to deal with most of these behind the scenes. Like any good father, He allowed me the time to process the areas in my life that were broken and sinful. Grace and mercy stepped in when I knew I didn't deserve it. God filled me with the power to overcome the things that kept me from being a vessel that He could use. He allowed me to see myself the way He created me and reassured me that He had chosen me. He forgave me and gave me the confidence that He still wanted to use me. His gifts came without repentance. Even when I wasn't living my life according to His standards, my purpose never went away. Even still, He didn't take His goodness away from me. He knew the truth of who I was even when I didn't. He knew my heart wanted to please Him.

Sometimes we can allow the judgment of others to limit us from fulfilling our purpose, and we'll ask ourselves self-defeating questions like: Can God really use me? What will people say? Will I be portrayed as a hypocrite? I remember when I struggled with these limiting thoughts as well. It's the reason I was too embarrassed to walk in my purpose. Please allow my testimony to help you with where you are. Maybe you aren't as messed up as I was, or perhaps you are. No matter what, your purpose is still waiting for you. The more I started to read the Bible, I discovered many great men and women who had character flaws. Everyone can have a story of redemption. Abraham was a liar, Jacob was a schemer, Rahab was a fornicator, David was an adulterer and murderer. But despite their character flaws, God still used them. This is why it's so essential for you to pursue your purpose despite your past. There are women and men in this world that need you to break free and become delivered from the pain of your past so that you can impact their lives. Had I never forgiven myself for my mistakes, I could have never helped Tracy.

You're a "Good Thing"

God intricately and specifically formed you and created you while you were in your mother's womb. Before she even knew you were there, He was behind the scenes creating you to be just the way you are. If you know anything about God, you know that He doesn't do anything by accident, and He surely doesn't do anything just because. When He makes something, He looks back and says that it's good. When He made you, He created a 'good thing.' But do you honestly feel that way about yourself? Or are you often complaining about your imperfections, dissatisfied with yourself, and how you were created. I often wonder how the lack of appreciation of ourselves affects God, especially when we treat His creation as if what He has done wasn't good enough. I believe that it hurts God when we don't appreciate the beautiful and purposeful beings we are.

My children love to create custom arts and crafts for me. I can always tell when they are making something special because they tell me things like, "Mommy, don't go in my room because there is a surprise for you." Less than an hour later, they will walk towards me with one hand behind their back, wearing a slight smirk on their faces. I always acknowledge my appreciation for them going out of their way to make something special for me. A hug and kiss generally follow with a big smile of thanks.

But how would that scene play out in a scenario where my eight-year-old daughter gave me the artwork that she had been working on so diligently, and I responded with, "I don't like it." Wouldn't my response crush her spirit? Do you think Winter would feel good about her creation? Do you think she would be willing to make me something else when she felt inspired? It also seems like a rude response, wouldn't you agree? But isn't this what we do to God when we compare ourselves to others wishing we had their gifts, talents, and seemingly perfect lives? Isn't this the same response we give to Abba Father when we tell Him what He's done in us just doesn't measure up to what He has done in others? Of course, you probably won't say this to Him verbatim; you don't need to. Your actions speak louder than your words.

I won't entirely put the pressure on you for all of the negative feelings you may entertain about yourself – there is a root cause to your disposition. Everything around you screams that what you have isn't good enough compared to what **others** have. We are filled with images in media that feed us the lie that if we change who we are, we would be more acceptable. It's sickening how we've been affected by what society has deemed to be worthy. Have you ever questioned why do we give so much weight in our lives to these false realities? Why does society (whoever he or she may be) have a voice for the masses? Who's setting the standard for society? It's the thought of inadequacy that keeps us from living our best life on purpose. You must change your perspective and accept how significant your purpose is before you can give birth. I can't emphasize enough the importance of what you are birthing. Although you may not have figured it out just yet, your lack of acknowledgment doesn't change the fact that it is there.

To live a life of purpose, you will need to shift your perspective about who you are and why you have been called to do what you do. Doing this will allow you to fully embrace yourself in the greatness in which you were created. Remember, your purpose is your life's work, and it's not just about you. It's about the influence and impact you will have on others. Shifting your perspective will keep you in perfect alignment with your life's work. We are all a part of this vast electric grid, and each one of us has a role to play to make sure there is light on the earth. In fact, Jesus called us the light of the world.

My least favorite part of the Christmas holiday is fishing for the lights to decorate the tree. I love decorating for Christmas, but I hate detangling the lights. Each year when we bring them out of the garage, without fail, no matter how much time we'd previously spent neatly packing the lights when we retrieve them, they are in a mangled mess. It takes so much time to straighten them out. After all of the hassle, when we finally get them unwrapped and plug them in, it's upsetting when they don't work because one of the lights has been blown. That one light affects the rest of the lights. One blown light bulb stops the entire string of lights from working.

I see our human electric grid the same way. If one of us fails to 'light up,' it affects the rest of us. Your purpose is that light. When you shift your perspective about your purpose, you will conclude that your purpose is not based on how worthy you think you are or you aren't. It's not based on your acceptance by others, and it's not based on other people's perceptions of you. You don't need validation from anyone. One of the things I admire about God is that He doesn't need the validation of others to use us for His Glory. In fact, it seems the least validated you are, the more He wants to use you. When you identify your purpose, you won't allow the lack of validation to hinder you. You'll be so focused on celebrating the gift that you are that you won't have time to entertain any negative messages that contradicts what God has told you about yourself.

Chapter II: Recap

- God chose you before the foundation of the world, and no matter what you have experienced up until this point, it doesn't change the fact that you are chosen.

- It will be difficult for you to accept your purpose until you first learn to accept that you being here is not an accident.

- Everyone can have a story of redemption.

- God intricately and specifically formed you and put you together while you were in your mother's womb.

- When you shift your perspective about purpose, you will conclude that your purpose is not based on how worthy you think you are or you aren't.

Chapter III

ARE YOU NAKED?

> "Who told you that you were naked?" the LORD God asked. "Have you eaten from the tree whose fruit I commanded you not to eat?"
> – Genesis 3:11

As I have stated previously, I have been deep diving into the subject of purpose for over seven years. Over time my knowledge has shifted as more revelation has been revealed to me through scripture. In my opinion, the subject of purpose is an ever-evolving topic. Although the core applications of pursuing your purpose will remain the same, as well as the mindset and willingness required to step out on faith – the process of how you will activate and walk in your pursuit of purpose will look different from what you see others do. There is no 'one size fits all' for your purpose. For one person, pursuing purpose may mean moving away from the familiar and venturing into uncharted territory to find their true calling. For another person, it may mean pursuing a life goal they have been too afraid to face because they failed at it once before. And for another, it may mean revisiting a painful life event. No matter what is necessary for you to personally pursue your purpose, you must do it. You must be willing to break free from the limitations that have been built around you that have limited your movement and growth.

As a society, we have been misinformed about how living a life of purpose should look. If you ingest the commentaries floating around about the topic, you'll probably feel inadequate or late to the party. You'll feel as if you are doing something wrong if you are not making a profit with your purpose. You'll believe that if you aren't sitting with a million dollars in your bank account, there must be something wrong with you. You'll think that if you don't have the life others say you should – then maybe you've missed God. These are all false perceptions of purpose.

Everyone is on a different level and trimester in their pursuit of purpose. Some women are in their first trimester, which is the 'Seeking and Discovery' level. These are the women learning their self-worth, value and digging up their layers to break through the strongholds of their past. This is a starting point for everyone in their pursuit of purpose. Some women are in the second trimester, which is the 'Vision Planning and Acceptance' level. They have gone through their Seeking and Discovery level, and now they understand what will be needed to walk in their purpose. And the last group is in the third trimester, the 'Birthing and Activation' level. This level is for those people who are in the labor and delivery room that are ready to push and be activated. We'll talk more in-depth about all three phases throughout the book.

To pursue purpose, you must first do the inner work to re-learn everything about yourself: your patterns, your quirks, your beliefs, your systems, and your triggers. The internal mirror is where many women remain stuck because doing the work on the inner you entails becoming truly honest and transparent with the root of your existence. This is where you must evaluate the recurring setbacks and self-sabotaging behaviors and accept your role in the story of your life, your relationships, your career, and your family. This is where you must ignore the outside noise and use your internal compass, and allow the Holy Spirit to guide you.

The Birthing Mirror

Let's begin unpacking your purpose by first examining the internal thoughts and emotions that you carry around with you every day. Think of this as the procedure in which the doctor uses an ultrasound to observe your baby. With the ultrasound, the doctor can determine how far along you are. It is too early to determine the sex of the baby or what you're carrying at this stage. Still, you will be able to experience the beginning of the birthing mirror as you use your internal mirror as the ultrasound.

What exactly is a birthing mirror? This is your open, honest, and transparent place. This is the place where you dive deep into the layers of your character and choices and evaluate how your life's circumstances have shaped you. This is the place where you reflect on your journey, who you are, what ideals define your life, and how you see yourself. In this place, you'll ask yourself introspective questions.

Look at the questions below and write out the thoughts that come to your mind as you read them aloud.

> Who am I, really?
>
> Am I living the life that I have dreamed of? If no, what is limiting me?
>
> Do I see myself as fearfully and wonderfully made? If no, how old was I when I stopped seeing myself this way?
>
> What were the circumstances surrounding the shift in my perspective of myself?
>
> How did that incident change my life?
>
> What has my life taught me so far?
>
> Can I reprogram my mind to see myself as God sees me?
>
> Do I see myself as worthy enough to live a life of purpose?

These are the questions I want you to truthfully answer. Respond to them according to every period of your life, including where you are today. I know this may seem more like a therapy session, and you may be asking, "How does this help me with pursuing my purpose?" Without a deep dive into the subject, I will explain it this way. To identify a tree, you must know what's planted in the ground or the soil. Seeds grow and bear fruit. Your purpose is a seed. You were impregnated with a seed when you entered the earth. This notion can be tested with the first woman Eve. In Genesis 1:28, she was given direction about her purpose in the garden.

> "Be fruitful, and multiply, and replenish the earth, and subdue it: and have dominion over the fish of the sea, and over the fowl of the air, and over every living thing that moveth upon the earth."

I would dare to say that as God is the Creator of the universe, He would know that the only thing that can bear fruit is a seed. So if He commanded us to be **fruitful** and **multiply**, it would lead me to understand that purpose is a seed. The birthing of your purpose is the production of your seed. The harvest of your purpose is the legacy that you leave on the earth – the testament that you lived a life of purpose.

Whatever is planted inside of you will grow. Now, this wouldn't be a bad thing if you were only carrying the seeds God gave you. However, we know this is not the case. As you have lived on this earth, some not-so-good seeds have been planted inside of you. These seeds are the experiences of life that leave a negative impact on how you see yourself. These are the seeds that make you fearful of the thought of rejection or failing before you even try. These are the seeds that stop you from trusting the process or accepting that God wants the best for you.

> "The kingdom of Heaven is like a man who sowed good seed in his field. But while everyone was sleeping, his enemy came and sowed weeds among the wheat and went away. When the wheat sprouted and formed heads, then the weeds also appeared. The owner's servants came to him and said, 'Sir, didn't you sow good seed in your field? Where then did the weeds come from?' 'An enemy did this,' he replied. "The servants asked him, 'Do you want us to go and pull them up?' 'No,' he answered, 'because while you are pulling the weeds, you may uproot the wheat with them." – Matthew 13: 24-29, NIV

The growth of the wheat (good seed) and weed (bad seed) explains what has happened inside you. The bad and good seeds have grown together, and some of the bad seeds have even grown into trees. Thankfully, a tree isn't permanent. You can always chop it down and pull up the roots. During your inner examination, you must be willing to uproot and destroy any idea formed because of the harmful and toxic situations that occurred in your life, no matter how insignificant it may have seemed at the time. If you don't address these underlying negative fruits, they will limit how you see yourself and keep you in a box. Instead of pursuing your purpose, you'll find yourself going into cycles making excuses as to why now isn't a good time for you. The core of who you are will determine how far you will or will not go.

The Fat Girl

My weight has always fluctuated since I was a little girl. My fight with obesity began when Motherdear fattened me up one summer with her Georgian southern-style cooking. I couldn't have been much older than seven years old when I started eating fried fish, grits, and homemade biscuits for breakfast, followed by fried chicken, collard greens with ham hocks, rice, and gravy for lunch. Throughout the day, I helped myself to homemade pound cakes and hand-churned vanilla ice cream. Let's just say I enjoyed myself that summer! But when the summer months were over, they almost had to roll me out of her house. As you can imagine, my metabolism slowed down tremendously.

My world quickly changed as I realized I had become the fat kid. I went from being the pretty little girl that everyone always complimented to having to shop for my clothes in the pretty plus section of the Sears department store. The compliments started to slow up, and people started treating me differently. My self-esteem quickly diminished because I didn't look like the other girls in my class, and I felt inadequate. It was years later that those feelings of inadequacy resurfaced. I noticed it the most when a relationship with a boy went sour. Instead of seeing the entire picture, I felt it was because I was too fat that the boys weren't attracted to me. When I finally landed my first boyfriend, he eventually dumped me for another girl. Those seeds of rejection started to grow with each new experience. Unknowingly I was watering seeds that the enemy sought to destroy me and keep me from my purpose.

During the Seeking and Discovery level, I had to revisit those earlier years of my life. I had to admit that feelings of insecurity and low self-esteem were planted at the root of my tree. I was married with kids before I finally revisited those memories. My actions in business, my inconsistency in life, and my fear of commitment all stemmed from those toxic thoughts I had about myself. My purpose could not be revealed until I was willing to accept, release, and forgive.

Are You Naked?

The Garden of Eden is one of those stories that resonates so much with me. Two individuals with perfect lives were tricked into believing that the things that God had given them were not good enough. They ate the fruit that caused them to see themselves from a negative perspective and lose their place with God. Let's move from the garden for just a moment and think about how this applies to you. I just opened up to you about the challenges I had with my weight and how it affected how I viewed myself. Those feelings can easily be attributed to my experiences with my nakedness.

Think about those naked moments that occurred in your life that have caused you to doubt and question who you really are. These are the doubts that replay in your mind just as you convince yourself you are ready to fulfill your purpose. These toxic thoughts that you have about yourself resurface and delay you from moving forward. Deep down inside, you know you've been called to live a fulfilled life of purpose, but you find yourself settling for less than you know you deserve. Can I ask you the question that God asked Adam? Who told you that you were naked? Nakedness, in this instance, means that you are ill-equipped with everything necessary to fulfill your purpose. Let's pick up on the conversation where Adam covered himself with fig leaves after God called for him. When he presented himself, God asked him in Genesis 3:11, "Who told you that you were naked?" I can imagine that God wanted to slap him in the back of the head and admonish him with some harsh words, but He's God, so of course He was careful with what He said. While reading and meditating on those seven strong words, I came to my own interpretation of how the scene played out after the cameras stopped rolling. I can hear the Almighty Father saying, "If you are taking your direction from Me, then why do you believe what you heard from an outsider's voice? You know my voice. You and I have a relationship. Why would you choose to ignore what I told you and attempt to do this on your own?" We know how the Adam and Eve story ended up. But what if you were in their situation? Would you have handled things differently?

The enemy's assignment is to convince you that it's too late or that you've missed out on your purpose. He wants you to believe that you've missed the train and that it will never come back around for you. He wants you to think that because you were a teenage mother, you endured a divorce, you experienced a physically abusive relationship, you flunked out of college, or you filed for bankruptcy – that

God can't use you, or it's too late for you. This is simply not true. One of Satan's tactics is to sabotage the thoughts we have about ourselves. He knows that our thoughts become our actions and our beliefs. Proverbs 23: 7 states, 'As a man thinketh in his heart, so is he.' He knows that once you begin to walk in doubt and question yourself, he can defeat you. He knows that he will win if he can shift your perception of how you see yourself instead of the way God created you.

Like many people, I allowed my past mistakes to halt me from moving towards my destiny. I fell into the trap, just like Eve did in that garden. I hope you can see where all of this naked talk is taking us. Truthfully, there is probably something in your life that you've done that has caused you to feel guilt and shame. This is the perfect time for you to accept what happened, take responsibility for your actions, forgive yourself, and see yourself through new lenses. The way to do this is to silence your negative voice, silence the negative voices of others, and silence the voice of the enemy. Any negative influence must be silenced. Because of the choices made in the garden, we'll always struggle with seeing ourselves the way God sees us. This is why we must look at our life's purpose from a different perspective – through different lenses. My prayer is that you'll trust the process of birthing your purpose. To do so, you must see yourself as well equipped, worthy, and deserving of the fulfillment of the promise. To get there, you'll need to have a vision for your life. This is crucial for your breakthrough.

Where Did the Lies Begin?

I was vulnerable with you earlier in this chapter, and now I want you to be open and honest with yourself. Go back and re-read the questions in this chapter. Process your deep inner reflections and write out where all the lies started for you. When did you first believe that your dreams were impossible? Who crushed you and left you for dead? Now I must ask you, are you ready to release the lies they told you? Are you ready to accept the truth of who God created you to be? When I work with my clients, I have them complete a life map that chronicles their life events. Doing this exercise forces them to take a trip down memory lane and face their best and worst moments. Once you clearly see life-altering moments and accept them, you can move on.

Inner Reflections:

Reflect on a time in your life when negative seeds were planted at the root of your Purpose Tree. I want you to process through those emotions that the incident evokes. Doing so will bring you closer to the reality of your purpose. Answer these questions:

- What life-altering situation(s) caused you to think differently about yourself?

- How does the memory of the incident(s) make you feel?

- What type of emotion(s) resurface at the memory?

- Has the incident(s) caused you to struggle with the beliefs that you have about yourself? If so, what are the negative beliefs that were planted?

- Has it been a hindrance to your growth? Do you find yourself constantly repeating and rehearsing the negative memories?

- What did you learn about yourself from that situation?

- How can you shift that experience as a life lesson to help others?

- Is there more internal work you need to process within yourself to understand how amazing you are?

It's Not Always Your Fault

Throughout this chapter, I have frequently mentioned taking personal accountability. Let me also say that every harmful tree or root in your life was not your fault. We suffer from some experiences due to the enemy using another person to inflict harm on us, especially in situations that result in sexual, physical, and mental trauma. God doesn't expect us to take responsibility for the actions of anyone else. Our responsibilities are to release, forgive, and protect ourselves (if possible) from being hurt by that person or any other offender again. I have coached women through some of the most challenging memories and experiences of their past. From rape to verbal abuse to domestic abuse, and the list of trauma goes on from there. It always breaks my heart to see women suffer for years, especially when what happened to them was out of their control. These experiences and memories are not easy for anyone to overcome and sweep under the rug. I get it, and even knowing this, I have to tell you that you must forgive. If you don't forgive, you will never be able to move forward into your divine purpose.

Forgive Yourself First, Then Forgive Others

Not only do you need to forgive others, but you need to forgive yourself. We tend to be extremely hard and judgmental of ourselves when it comes to our personal decisions. We sometimes carry around years of anger against ourselves because of the choices we made in our lives. Always remember that forgiving and healing first start from within.

One day I was listening to my husband minister a message about the importance of forgiveness. He stressed how unforgiveness is a sin that will keep you out of Heaven. The Bible tells us if we don't forgive others, God can't forgive us. Do you think God will open Heaven's doors to you if you don't forgive others? Sadly, the answer to that question is no. The release of the hurt and pain is necessary before purpose can be fulfilled in your life. As you chew on this a bit, it is a good time for you to ask the Holy Spirit to reveal to you if there is any unforgiveness in your heart. Take out a sheet of paper and write out every person and incident that comes to your mind as the Spirit unfolds them. Trust me, it's not worth you missing out on your purpose because you can't release the hurt. Don't give them or it that much power over you.

When you finish this list, say this out loud:

(Complete this activity for each person on your list, including yourself.)

_____ *(name)* I forgive you and I am releasing _____ *(the incident)* today.

There is an urgency for you to walk in God's love and forgiveness. You're pregnant and time is of the essence. I urge you to never forget that someone is waiting for you to show them how to overcome a similar struggle that you have endured. Your ability to see yourself the way God sees you will propel you to go from being a victim to a warrior.

Now that you have looked at yourself through the birthing mirror, I want you to see yourself in the exterior mirror. When you look into your eyes, I want you to see your strength. I want you to see your survival and how that translates into you walking in your purpose. The enemy of your soul has been feeding you lies about your past. He's been trying to make you feel as if what God has given you – what He placed on the inside of you – is not enough. Don't fall into the trap. Before you proceed to the next chapter, take some time to review the questions in this chapter. Think about how answering the questions made you feel. Take an honest assessment of your emotions. After you do this, determine if you are ready to proceed further or if there is more internal work for you to do. Understanding your purpose is not an overnight process. It's not as simple as answering a few questions and circling the correct answer based on a scientific study. Discovering your purpose is much deeper than surface answers and responses. Once you have truly tapped into your understanding, you will use the revelation to share with the world. This is what you will use to help others discover purpose within themselves. This is the weight of your assignment.

Chapter III: Recap

- Everyone is on a different level in their pursuit of purpose.

- To pursue purpose, you must first do the inner work and learn everything about yourself: your patterns, your quirks, your beliefs, your systems, and your triggers.

- Purpose cannot be revealed until you are willing to accept, release, and forgive. If you don't forgive, you will never be able to move forward into your divine purpose.

- The core of who you are will determine how far you will or will not go.

- One of Satan's tactics is to sabotage the thoughts we have about ourselves. He knows that our thoughts become our actions and our beliefs.

Chapter IV

PREGNANT WITH PURPOSE

> *But I have raised you for this very purpose, that I might show you my power and that my name might be proclaimed in all the earth.*
> *– Exodus 9:16*

OPS! I THINK I missed my last two menstrual cycles, and I should probably take a pregnancy test just to be safe. This was my thought after five years into my marriage when I noticed something was happening in my body. Instead of speculating any further, I purchased an EPT digital pregnancy test at the grocery store. I secretly made my way to the bathroom at home, hoping not to alarm my husband. I opened the box, careful not to damage the test inside, and plopped down on the side of the tub and read the instructions. I followed the instructions, placed the test on the counter, and waited for the results. I watched it quickly change, and before the two minutes had elapsed, there was a blue cross shining brightly, indicating that we were about to become parents. Excited and nervous, I ran into the kitchen to share the news with my husband, who had no idea that I was even taking the test. "We're pregnant!" I blurted out. He smiled with a slight nervousness on his face as he hugged me.

The fears began to kick in almost immediately after discovering that I was pregnant. I was happy with the idea, but I wasn't convinced that I could handle the responsibilities of being a mommy. I was in my early thirties, and although my husband and I occasionally spoke about having a child, I wasn't prepared to have my entire world changed forever. This sounds utterly selfish as I write this, but this is a no-judgment zone, right? I admit that I wasn't the motherly type. I had a college friend who I always teased because she dreamed of being a wife and mother. She not only purchased bridal magazines at every grocery checkout, but she had a list of the names of her future children. She dreamed of the Cinderella wedding and the perfect family. She was prepared while I, on the other hand, was the complete opposite – a free spirit that wanted to live a life with little responsibilities.

Quite honestly, I don't know too many people who are fully prepared to take on the challenges of raising a human being. We like the idea of having a baby, and we love the sweet baby smell and cute clothes, but sometimes secretly, we want to send them back at the end of the day. I was satisfied with being the cool aunt. The one that feeds the kids ice cream and cake and sends them home to their parents with a sugar high at the end of the night. Children, as cute as they are, require a lot of work. Trust me, I know, I now have three (who I wouldn't trade for the world – by the way).

When we first married, I expressed to my husband that I wanted to have a kid-free life. I wanted to do me. I had just tipped my toe back in the acting world and had hopes of one day landing it big in New York City. I had performed on local stages throughout Florida – my mind was set on entertainment. After the wedding, I was planning to take my acting even more seriously. I never had a chance to do that, and now we were having a baby. The panic and fear, and questions all swarmed my mind at once. *Can we do this? Where will we get the extra money to care for a baby? Will I need to quit working on my business? Is everything going to change?* I worried about the timing of bringing this new baby into the world. But despite my fears, the reality was a little one was on the way.

Carrying a Baby Compared to Carrying Purpose

Being pregnant has a way of changing you. I was conscious about everything, including my emotional breakdowns, because I read that the baby could feel what I was feeling. I was careful not to overload myself with junk food. I wanted to do all I could to ensure my baby received the proper nutrients he needed to grow healthy and strong inside me. I became very cautious of who touched my belly and of people smoking around me. I also monitored his little kicks to make sure that he was safe inside. Under my watch, there was nothing I wouldn't do to protect the growing baby inside of me.

My natural pregnancy gave me insight into what it means to be pregnant with purpose. Carrying purpose requires the same sort of attention, care, and gentleness as having a baby. You must protect your purpose from any hostile environments that are not conducive to a healthy delivery. You also must monitor what you eat mentally, emotionally, and spiritually because anything you do can affect the growth and delivery of your purpose.

Do you realize that you have been carrying something so great that God allowed it to be hidden from you until you were ready to accept it? There is greatness inside you, but I am sure this is not new information to you. You have always known that you were different, as you think differently than the people in your family and your co-workers. You're always coming up with innovative concepts and ideas; you usually think outside the box. This is why you are becoming even more uncomfortable remaining in your current state. This discomfort has caused your awakening, as you have been experiencing newness in your vision for your life. Your appetite for things and people is changing, and you are no longer interested in the things that used to draw you. Your purpose is growing inside of you, and it is causing a shift in your mindset.

There is a supernatural preparation that takes place before you birth your purpose. I recognized the changes that were occurring in my life when I was carrying my purpose.

I started to get a twinkle in my eye and a pep in my step. I couldn't think about anything else but starting my new project. I no longer wanted to waste time with people that weren't having any success in life. I no longer desired to gossip about people and what they were doing and who they were doing it with. I no longer wanted to talk about change, but I really desired to become a better me in every area. I was willing to do the work to become the best version of myself, and I felt alive again. The empty feeling of *'why was I on this earth'* started to subside.

Purpose and Destiny Collide

In 2015, I was contracted to coordinate a five-city tour for a Prophetic women's conference. My client was a mighty woman of the faith, and I quickly caught hold of her vision and promised to make her event the best conference that she and her guests would ever experience. I went into full planning mode covering every area of the event, even those that weren't in the scope of my contracted work. I was always one of those overachieving event planners that covered things that didn't even involve me; sometimes, it worked out in my favor; other times, I regretted sticking my nose in something that didn't involve me. The time for the Chicago tour stop finally came, and my husband and I arrived at the hotel to set up everything that was needed. I had my checklists, and I made sure that my duties were completed.

I sprinted across the room during the event as women were prayed for and hands were laid on them. I stood close to the event host, making sure to be there when she needed me.

I moved shoes, passed out Kleenex tissues, and held women as they cried while having their breakthrough moments. I monitored the event timeline, cued the psalmist, and worked out the kinks with the hotel management and staff behind the scenes. I didn't want to drop the ball or interrupt the flow of the Holy Spirit, and by the end of the two-day event, I was very exhausted.

At the conference, an older lady caught my attention with her warm smile. After she greeted me, she told me that she needed to speak with me. "Okay, no problem," I responded. I didn't know who she was at the time or why she wanted to talk to me. Sometime later, the event host introduced her as a well-respected woman of God. Towards the wrap-up, she realized that I would never get a breather until I was completely packed up, and my client had retired for the night. The nice lady cornered me and declared, "God is going to use you mightily. And although you are here serving, He is bringing you to the forefront. Your days of serving others behind the scenes are limited." I really didn't know how to receive her message, but I thanked her for her words, and I moved on to finish the event. I honestly did not give much thought to what she had said.

God had shown her something about me that He hadn't even revealed to me. In my eyes, I was a servant first and anything else after. I had worked at church conferences for years working with special guests, handling their seating, and carrying their Bibles when necessary. I had fixed my share of hot tea and iced water for over five-plus years, and

I never knew anything else but service. I had no idea that God was grooming me for the front row; truthfully, that was the farthest thing from my mind. I didn't know God was watching how faithfully I would serve before he would elevate me. I thought I was just doing a good deed of service to my pastors, and I never expected anything in return. As I have grown in my faith walk, I now know better. God was watching my heart to see if I would be a good steward over a small capacity. He watched how I handled His people. He carefully evaluated whether He could trust me to be faithful to show up with a smile and stay on my post until my job was done and until the last special guest was whisked away in the black Lincoln at the end of the night.

For many years, I had extensive experience in having a front-row seat as others who seemed more gifted and qualified than I, was living what appeared to be their best life. Often, I would watch in amazement as presenters would deliver keynote speeches and be in awe of how eloquently their words seamlessly came together. I stood in the background while they were speaking, taking notes in the shadows. It was similar to babysitting my siblings without the experience of actually giving birth. I was the person that everyone called on to serve on a hospitality committee or volunteer to help backstage at a conference. Never allowed to play in the game, but made sure the team's equipment, water and towels were in place. It didn't bother me at all. It genuinely bought me pleasure to see others shine in their spotlight. I was always very secure and didn't consider myself less than just because I served others. In all transparency, some people I helped thought of me as less than. Sadly, it was a few fellow believers in the faith. I could always tell by the way they spoke to or addressed me. Even though I chose not to keep score, **God did.**

I Think I'm Pregnant!

Shortly after that encounter in Chicago, I began to feel uneasiness and a fire inside of me, pushing me to produce my own women's conference. At that point, I had been planning other leader's events for over seven years, and I saw a need in the marketplace for events that inspired mothers and children at the same time. I was new to Houston, and having small children in a new environment without support made me wonder how many others were like me who also had difficulty finding a babysitter and a support system while running their business.

It would be great to say that I had a mentor who coached me in how to plan and coordinate all the details of organizing my own event, as I was venturing into new territory, but yeah – not quite. It's almost as if God kept me isolated so He could personally coach me. Trust me, I am all for business and life coaches; I coach many women through my business endeavors. But sometimes, the Holy Spirit wants to be your only teacher, with no other outside voices influencing you. This is what my pregnancy of purpose entailed – learning to trust God's voice.

I have given you quite a bit to digest here, and you may not be sure if you're pregnant with purpose. I want to take this time to provide you with a quick (pregnancy) checkup, and if you answer 'yes' to any or all of these statements, then yes, you're pregnant!

1. You feel miserable where you are in life; you know there has to be more for you.
2. You dream about a life different from where you are today, and you have a glimmer of hope that it's possible.
3. You are passionate about a particular cause, and you see little to nothing being done to effect change, and it frustrates you.
4. People are constantly coming up to you asking you if you carry a particular title or if you are a professional.
5. You have received similar recurring prophecies spoken over your life by various people who often don't know one another.
6. You have recurring dreams and visions of a better life.

Answering the Call

There were questions about how this new life would affect my lifestyle, as I didn't have formal training in teaching others. I had learned my life skills, but no degree or certificate qualified me to help train and birth others to walk in their purpose. But even still, day after day, God reassured me that He had called me for this purpose.

I wrestled with the idea of how and why God wanted to use me. *Why is God calling me out of my comfort zone? How can I help others when I often still struggle to know myself? Can I get more time to prepare? Help! I'm not ready.* Some months after that encounter at the conference, there was a pulling in my spirit that God was calling me to do more for Him and serve others. As a child of a pastor, there was never a personal desire for me to enter into ministry. I felt that ministry didn't fit my lifestyle. I had seen the labor of love required, and it didn't fit into the grand scheme of my vision for my life. Of course, God wasn't consulted about my decision, and no matter how far I distanced myself, someone somewhere would have a need that I would be cornered into ministering to.

Unknowingly, my purpose laid dormant, patiently waiting as it took me some time to accept who I was. As you read this, can you think of that thing you know deep down inside that you've been called to do, but you dread the amount of time and effort it will take to fulfill it? Let me advise you as lovingly as I can. You won't be fulfilled until you accept your call. A growing belly makes any pregnant woman uncomfortable, and so does a growing purpose. Sometimes there is a fear that can overtake us when we think about those goals that are out of our natural reach. I have said it before, and I will repeat it- the how's and what's are not your responsibility. You just need to accept the call and then put one foot in front of the other as God orders your steps. Trust me, He has enough influence and power to send the people you need in your path to help you develop, birth, and steward your purpose.

The Call to Action

There was a need in the marketplace for business events that catered to women and children, which would train them spiritually and naturally and prepare families to create a financial legacy. I couldn't get it out of my mind – the vision was so clear. The result of that was the birthing of the 'Mommy and Me Dream Bigger Tour.' I had no idea of how or what I would do; I just knew it aligned with my purpose.

It first started inwardly with a desire to become closer to God. Before working at the conference in Chicago, there was a burning desire to fast and pray more and spend more time in His presence. I started to long for a deeper understanding of who He was, and in return, He started showing me things about myself that were packed away and hidden for years. Entering this quest for self-discovery and revelation of my purpose resulted in me spending hours sitting with a pen, paper, and worship music softly playing in the background, writing down whatever was dropped into my spirit. I created an intimate atmosphere for Him to talk to me as I listened. I loved sitting in His presence as those moments created an atmosphere conducive to the birthing of purpose.

In this intimate place of worship, I uncovered the real Sherrie. I was vulnerable and transparent with the challenges I was facing and strongholds bigger than I could handle. As He prepared me for the birthing of purpose, I became the seven-year-old Sherrie. She didn't need to be like the women who appeared to have it all together when she was truly broken inside. It was a safe place, and I could address my fears and disappointments without any judgments. During my devotion time, the areas that I still struggled with were revealed. These were the 'small sins' that were necessary for me to repent and grow. He showed me my insecurities and the fears I had of failure. He showed me the areas that I still carried bitterness, unforgiveness, and hurt. He showed me how I truly wanted acceptance from others, although I adamantly denied it. He showed me how shame had stifled my ability to be the best version of myself. He showed me all of me.

> **As the deer pants for streams of water, so my soul pants for you, my God. My soul thirsts for God, for the living God. When can I go and meet with God? –Psalms 42:1-2 NIV**

Being pregnant with purpose will cause you to hunger for righteousness. The Bible gives us so many references about His desire for us to draw near to Him and delight in Him (James 4:8, Psalms 37:4). The Psalmist David was a huge worshipper that spent hours in the presence of God. He longed to be with the Father, and because of this, he was labeled 'a man after God's own heart.' David won many wars and gained much insight as he worshipped. One of the benefits of being in God's presence is that He speaks, leads, and directs. He led me during each step of the pursuit of my purpose, delicately revealing the blueprint for my life.

Giving birth to purpose is the manifestation of the promises that God has for you. As you grow and evolve, so does your assignment. As you pass one level, you will experience the opportunity to ascend to the next. As a child, I learned that prayer was simply talking to our Creator, so doing that was easy. Listening - well, that was a different story. There was a part of me that spoke more than I listened. Learning to listen more and talk less had to become a developed trait. Quite honestly, it is challenging to receive direction if you are doing all of the talking. When women tell me they don't hear God speaking to them, I quickly ask them, "are you talking or are you listening?" This is an intricate part of your breakthrough to your purpose. You must be able to accurately hear directions without any distractions.

Watch Your Baby Leap

One of the joys of pregnancy is feeling your baby kick in your belly. It's a feeling a new mother can't explain, and it's also a reassurance that everything is still okay on the inside. As you prepare to give birth to purpose, you should also connect with others that are also pregnant. These connections will cause your baby to leap and encourage you during your process. You may be wondering how you can find others that are also pregnant? Don't worry – you'll recognize them. They'll be the ones asking questions, being accountable, and taking responsibility for their lives and decisions. They'll be the ones that are focused and disciplined with little time for distractions. When you meet them, they'll have a glow and a passion for life. I love reading about Mary and her cousin Elizabeth in the Bible and their babies that leaped within their bellies when they met up with each other to share the good news. When you encounter women that are pregnant in the spirit, your baby will leap. You'll get excited and want to share your experiences. I meet quite a few women, but there are some people that I connect with almost immediately, and when we begin talking, it's as if we've known each other for years. Often we're sharing testimonies and war stories, and we get so excited that before we know it, we've been on the phone well over an hour. That's how it feels when you connect with like-minded women who are carrying purpose. When you surround yourself with others that are pregnant, it will keep you more conscious of your environment and choices.

Being pregnant with purpose is a beautiful experience. Enjoy your growth, don't rush the process. During this time, prepare yourself for the take-off. Prepare your environment as a mother preparing a room for her baby. Make any adjustments and get rid of the things that no longer serve you. Everything about you is changing- don't fight it.

Chapter IV: Recap

- Carrying purpose requires the same sort of attention, care, and gentleness as having a baby does. You must protect your purpose from any negative environments that are not conducive to a healthy delivery.

- You must monitor what you eat mentally, emotionally, and spiritually. Anything you do can affect the growth and delivery of your purpose.

- Sitting in God's presence creates an atmosphere that is conducive for the womb and birthing of purpose.

- You won't be fulfilled until you accept your call. A growing belly makes any pregnant woman uncomfortable, and so does a growing purpose.

- As you prepare to give birth to purpose, connect with others that are also pregnant.

Chapter V

FOLLOW THE PATH TO PURPOSE

> *Moses answered, "What if they do not believe me or listen to me and say, 'The Lord did not appear to you'?" Then the LORD asked him, "What is that in your hand?" – Exodus 4:2, NIV*

IT'S PROBABLY EVIDENT AT this point in the book that I have a deep passion for helping women discover their purpose. In fact, for most women I meet, I encourage them to find out who they are outside of the roles and titles they wear. I challenge my married friends to rediscover those inner dreams they had before they became a wife. I push those moms to remember the goals they had before their life became immersed in motherhood. We've been blessed to experience these roles for a reason. They help to shape us and mature us into the women we are today. Until I became a mother, I didn't have a proper understanding of what it meant to love unconditionally. My life changed the day I gave birth. But even with all of the beautiful life lessons I have learned as a wife and mother, I am still Sherrie, the little girl with purpose.

As women, it's easy for us to lose ourselves in our titles and neglect the inner girl inside of us, who is longing to find her place in the world. This is a disservice not only to you but it's a disservice to your Creator. Discovering my purpose was a lot like the discovery and evolution of my pregnancy with my first child. It crept up on me because I wasn't planning for it, neither had I prepared for it. But once I knew I was pregnant, I went into full research mode with reading and preparation. According to my terms, the timing wasn't perfect, but God knew just what I needed and when I needed it.

When you decide to unlock your purpose and start moving forward, you'll discover a road filled with twists, turns, and plots. Don't allow that uncertainty to discourage you and cause you to retreat because learning who you are is a process. It's not a complicated process, but it is a process. When you are ready to walk in your purpose, your first stop is Seeking and Discovery. This is your self-realization and understanding of where your personality, character traits, and habits began. The discovery process requires inner work. During my Seeking and Discovery process, I realized that purpose had been showing up all my life, for well over thirty years, but somehow I had missed it. I had dismissed the things that brought me joy and the moments that I never wanted to end. Buried under the cares of life were the dreams I had as a little girl. I uncovered the underlying fears, which allowed me to remove the blockages to enjoy the healing and restoration that would follow. The path reassured me that I wasn't insane when I went against the grain or when I thought outside of the boxes that others had built for me. It bought clarity as to why I never fit in with the popular crowds or why I often saw things from a different perspective. It felt good to get in touch with the authentic me. I had lost myself for over a decade, and finding myself again was a feeling that I can't explain. It was liberating.

The Holy Spirit began to take me down a journey that I called the 'Pursuit of Purpose.' During my devotion times, He started to reveal things about myself to me. I listened as He prompted me with pertinent questions that led me down the path of purpose. These seemed like difficult questions at the time, but the reflection led me closer to unlocking my calling.

> Do you know who you are?
> Do you know why you were created?
> Do you know the strengths of your personality?
> Do you know how you can use these traits to help others?

These were a few of the questions that caused me to sit, think, and dig deeper. I want to challenge you to reflect on these questions as well. As you sit in a still and calm place, allow the Holy Spirit to minister to you and bring you clarity.

When I began asking God the right questions, He revealed the hidden treasures on the inside of me. He showed me how my character traits were precisely what was needed to live out my calling. There was nothing additional that I needed; I had everything already inside of me. You are no different – the tools necessary to successfully fulfill your purpose are on the inside of you. Think about the character traits that you have buried or put away on the shelf. You may not have connected the dots, and this could be the reason why you haven't uncovered your purpose as of yet. But don't worry, your time of destiny is here. At the end of this journey, I want you to have clarity and be confident about what you are carrying. You need to know who you are and how you can fulfill the assignment that God has for you.

Your path to purpose will require you to assess where you are today and what you envision for your future. This becomes less about working in a job than running a business and more about choosing the right path that leads you to your destiny. Contrary to popular belief, everyone isn't meant to become a full-time business owner. People are needed to carry out their purpose in the different spheres and sectors that add value to our world in Corporate America, Nonprofit Organizations, and communities scattered across the earth. The question you should be asking yourself is, "Is what I am doing today leading me to the path of purpose?" Allow me to give you some clarity. If you are an accountant, but you desire to work with teenage moms to coach and lead them to a life of change and direction, then I can probably guess that you are not working on a path to purpose. If you are working as a leader or manager in Corporate America, and you know that you would like to coach and lead others to success, then where you are will most likely enhance your leadership capabilities and give you the hands-on training and expertise you need to succeed in this area. Where are you today in your life and career path? Is it leading you closer to a life of fulfillment?

During my junior year of high school, the counselor asked me what I wanted to do with my life after graduation. Based on that answer, a list of comparable occupations was given to me, and the suggested post-education study focus. Although there are exceptions, you will rarely know your purpose as a teenager. In our school-age years, I would say that you are less likely to know who you are and what you want to do with your life. Meeting with a counselor to choose a career path when you've only lived a fraction of your life will most likely include a limited list of matched occupations. Your choices will be based on your narrowed outlook on life.

I attribute a lot of sudden mid-life changes to this high school practice. Although the intention is good, the effects are harmful to the psyche of young people who are uncertain of where they fit in this world. One day they wake up and realize that the life they have been living is not what they want, and it isn't in alignment with who they are. They recognize they chose a life path based on how they felt during a different time in their life. This can be dangerous when this realization takes place much later in life because you end up burning a lot of bridges and even crippling the lives of the people closest to you. When I was younger, there was a family that experienced this. The mother, who had been the pillar of the family, decided she was leaving her husband and daughters because she was no longer happy within herself. The couple had been married for over a decade and was the picture-perfect image of a stable home environment. They served on the church committees, their girls were always neatly dressed, and every time we saw them, there were smiles on their faces. Her sudden departure ripped their family apart; it was years before the relationship with her daughters was repaired. She is an example of a woman who tried to find herself after she was already deeply intertwined in her life. I am not sure what conversations happened behind the doors of this family, but if she was anything like the women I meet today, she could have been caught in the Anti-Purpose Cycle of doing and not in the life of becoming.

The Big Move

The path to purpose will not always be as clear and specific as we want. But don't allow that to discourage you. Your calling will be presented to you like a jigsaw puzzle- piece by piece and on a need-to-know basis. The day my family and I moved to Houston was filled with so many mixed emotions. Before the move to Texas, I owned an event planning business in Miami. The company opened amazing doors for us financially and socially as we landed contracts with celebrities, luxury retail stores and won awards and various recognitions. We were on top and rising – or so I thought. But things began to quickly change, and I watched everything that we had built over five years come crashing down. My financial comfort was shaken, and almost overnight, it felt as if we had lost everything. *"How could this happen to me?"* I cried. Once the doors started to close, my family was directed to Houston, Texas, to begin life again.

We didn't know what to expect, but we were obedient to the Holy Spirit's leading, and there was an excitement for change in a new environment. This was a huge walk of faith that entailed a battle with the uncertainty of life, as the entire picture wasn't laid out for us. I questioned God quite a bit during this time. We were led to move to a new state with no friends, no job, and no connections. Sounds crazy, right? "Do you trust me? Are you willing to give me everything? Will you say yes?" These were the resounding questions I heard in my spirit.

We lived in a hotel room with three kids ages 1,3, and 5 years during the first year of the move. Many late nights and early mornings were spent in prayer and worship, as I desperately sought to find my place and understand how the move aligned with my divine assignment. For a control freak, this was torture. Not only did it challenge me to grow spiritually, but it caused me to grow as a woman, a wife, and a mother. After arriving at our Promised Land, like the Israelites, we had to fight the giants to possess what was promised to us. Those lean times taught me how to appreciate every blessing – big or small. It taught me to appreciate life and how to sit still and wait. The most precious asset I walked away with at the end of that experience was one I could never place a dollar value on; it was the understanding of my purpose and the truth of the value of who I was. I gained clarity of my seed traits, and I understood my gifts and how they worked hand in hand with my purpose. I understood why I thought the way I did and that it was okay to be me. I understood what I needed to do to fulfill my calling, and I understood my 'why.' I had my awakening – I had discovered my purpose.

Bringing the Pieces Together

Your purpose has been showing up in bite-sized portions throughout your life, like clues to a riddle. Years ago, I struggled with putting the clues together because my life was fragmented. Fragments are the things that are broken and leftover after someone breaks off the pieces they need. I was fragmented by life experiences, bad relationships, and past choices. While scrolling through YouTube one day, I came across a woman preaching about fragmented pieces. I sat there in tears as she explained how our lives constantly go into circles because of our negative spiritual and emotional experiences. That resonated with me deeply because it truly explained what I had been experiencing for over ten years. I noticed that the fragments were blocking me from getting to know the authentic me again. After being honest with my pain, I became open enough to receive the pieces to the puzzle and understand how they all worked together. Allow me to further explain how my life experiences led me to my purpose.

Life Experience - Teaching Children

During my teenage years, I was hired as a summer Bible Camp Counselor. The ten-week summer program placed me in front of elementary school students. I held that job position for a few summers. From there, I felt comfortable enough to teach cheerleading techniques to young girls at my church, using what I had learned as a cheerleader while on my high school cheer squad. As far back as I can remember, I have been in the front of the room teaching children, so it was a natural progression when I birthed the 'Mommy and Me Dream Bigger Conference' for moms and kids.

> **This life experience prepared me for one of my life's missions to connect with moms. It built my confidence as a speaker, which led to the birthing of my coaching business over time.**

Life Experience - Stage Performer

I was a theatrical stage performer from high school into my adult life. It was almost second nature for me to embrace a new character, memorize my lines, and perform in front of an audience. Fast forward, more than thirty years later, and I am on stage in a different arena. I travel around the world hosting speeches, workshops, and empowerment sessions. I may have a few butterflies, but overall I am not intimidated to stand in front of an audience and walk in my purpose.

Performing became a part of my life at an early age, and it's second nature for me to turn it on when needed. I had no idea when I started performing that it would be something I would be doing for my entire life. I knew at the time that I was passionate about it. I loved it, and I loved the way I felt when the endorphins were released during a performance. I didn't mind the countless hours it required for me to study, perfect my lines, or the hours it took to rehearse and immerse in my character. Those were great times, and I enjoyed that season of my life.

> **This life experience helped me to become comfortable as a professional speaker and taught me how to keep my audience engaged in my message.**

Life Experience – Leadership

In high school, I was elected class president of my senior class. It was a position of leadership that I occupied and never really appreciated as a 16-17-year-old girl. I ran for the position in all transparency because very few students wanted to fill the role, and I was encouraged by my school mentor. I gave it a shot because it came with many perks and benefits that would assist me when I applied to college. I had no idea how it felt to lead people. I quickly learned that leadership came with responsibilities, and not everyone would agree with me or even like me. This position also offered me an opportunity to write and deliver my first speech in an auditorium filled with 5000+ people at the age of 17 years.

Unbeknownst to me at that time, I had no idea that I would still be leading others more than 20 years later. This opportunity introduced me to my leadership gifting.

> **This experience helped me to identify my leadership skills, learn responsibility, and how to help others.**

Life Experience- Writer and Editor

During my time in college, I was offered my first editing opportunity by my pastor's wife. She was the Chief Administrator at the time and wanted to rewrite their employee handbook. I was intimidated at first, but being a risk-taker, I decided to go for it, and it also came with a nice-sized check. I am unsure why she chose me for that project, but she obviously saw something in me that I didn't. Completing that project gave me the confidence I needed to see myself as a writer. This continued to show up in other areas, as many times I was asked to rewrite my friends' papers or spruce up a letter before my parents mailed it out. From there, I became an editor of a local magazine and was asked to join a few writing teams for movie scripts and plays. People constantly complimented me on my writing ability and started to ask me to help them write their books. Years later, it felt natural when I started my publishing company and coaching programs to help professionals write their books.

> **This experience helped me to unlock my writing ability which led me to my purpose.**

Life Experience- Business Skills

As a side job to help pay for some of my college experiences, I worked in the retail section of the
New York & Company store. I learned so many skills while working in that job, for example, the art of customer service, presentation, and how to sell and upsell. I often placed first in the store sales per hour challenges and opening credit cards for customers. I learned how to fold a T-shirt and a pair of jeans precisely and the importance of merchandising. After a year of employment, I was promoted to Assistant Store Manager and was responsible for scheduling, bank drops, and register reconciliation. I didn't understand why that position was important until I opened my business ten years later, which required the incorporation of those skills.

> **This experience helped me discover and hone the skills needed to become a successful business owner.**

Life Experience- Starting Again

After relocating to the city of Houston, our family struggled financially. For the first time in my life, I had to apply for government assistance, and my children were on the free lunch program at school. We shopped with food stamps and relied on free school supplies and thrift stores to dress our children. This was a humbling experience for me, and it caused me to rely on the help of others to maintain a roof over our heads. I never would have imagined that this script would have been in my story. Now, I know God used that low time to teach me things about myself. Before that experience, I had a lot of pride, and I lacked empathy. If I saw someone struggling, I judged and assumed they had caused it on themselves or didn't want to do better. I ignorantly believed those that struggled financially didn't have dreams or a vision for their life. I had a false reality in relating to the struggles of people.

While I was going through my storm, my eyes were opened to others going through life's struggles. I started reading more and listening to teachings that built up my spirit man. I learned about Spiritual Warfare, and I became stronger in the fight for spiritual freedom. I learned how important it is to give back and offer a hand to those that are in need. I learned to stop looking at life through my selfish lens. Had you asked me two years before my move to Houston if I could see myself as being homeless and without money in the bank, I would have said that it would never happen to me. I had it all together, and I had my life figured out. But I am so glad now that I was able to experience struggles because they taught me how to be grateful for whatever I have. These lessons guide me as I help people from all walks of life find hope in desperate situations. Through this experience I learned how to create something from nothing and rebuild my life from the ground up. I learned that what I have on the inside is valuable. This experience also reassured me that I can survive and bounce back from anything.

This experience helped me find empathy for others, birth my ministry, and grow

spiritually and emotionally. It was the catalyst for my coaching and training programs and an introduction to our ministry.

Life Experience- International Expansion

While shopping for a client's event in an arts and crafts store in 2018, I had a brief thought on what it would be like to expand my brand on an international level. Silently, I whispered under my breath, "God, can you help me book a client in China?" and I continued shopping and didn't give it any more thought. Less than a week later, I woke up to alerts buzzing on my Facebook page. When I logged in to see what they were about, there was a conversation in one group, and I was tagged in the correspondence. A woman was looking to write her book, and a client that I had helped to write her book in 90 days recommended me for the job. I gave the woman a call and began asking her questions about her book project, as I usually do with an introductory call. When I asked her where she resided, she told me that she was a professor in Guangzhou, China. I could have dropped the phone in astonishment, as my eyes started to well up with tears of appreciation. I proceeded to tell her about my prayer and how God had connected us. We wrote her book, and I was able to fly to China for her book release. That one connection has opened countless doors for my business and my brand. Not only was this experience rewarding, but it also confirmed how much our Heavenly Father wants to give us the desire of our hearts.

> **This experience helped me to expand internationally and grow my business to a new market. It taught me not to be afraid to ask for what I want.**

These experiences are just some of the areas in my life that have helped steer me and aligned me with my purpose. Everything started as pieces to a puzzle: experiences, open doors, ideas, and passions – and now I can see how perfectly it all fits in my life. When I started my journey, I realized that I had forgotten many of my attributes and talents. The Seeking and Discovery process sent me on a journey that unlocked the memories of how life was in the past. I started pulling out old awards and accolades, and the amazing woman God created me to be, begin to shine through. The diamond in me had to be chiseled and polished to help me find myself.

My assignment is to help you connect your experiences with your life purpose. You've had a chance to review the pieces of my story; now, let me show you how they joined together to lead me to my purpose.

> **My purpose is to impact the lives of 1,000,000 women around the world. I will help them find their purpose and unlock their voices through my writings, business coaching, life coaching, family counseling, and professional speaking.**

Do you see how my experiences were the foundation of my mission? Do you see that my purpose is not about fulfilling my selfish ambitions but serving others? The proper alignment helps me to daily fulfill the assignment God has entrusted me with, and I declare that I will be a good steward.

Client Testimonial:

> *"To my publishing and writing coach, Dr. Sherrie Walton, thank you for giving me the tools needed to bring everything inside of my heart to life. Even during our initial conversation, God was speaking through you to me. I am so grateful for you and your obedience to your calling. You have forever changed my life in so many ways, and for that, I thank you."*
>
> *−Cortina Peters, Licensed Therapist, Clinical Social Worker, Best-Selling Author of The W.O.W. Effect*

Now think about your life experiences, both good and bad. Take some time to start writing them out. After you identify them, take a deeper introspection and ask yourself:

What are some of the essential experiences in my life?
What have I learned from those experiences?
How have these experiences led me to the direction of my purpose?

What are the experiences (personal, professional, and spiritual) I have endured that I can use as a tool to help someone else grow?

By now, you can begin to put some of your life puzzle pieces together. Take some time to meditate on this section.

Let's keep going.

Chapter V: Recap

- When you are ready to walk in your purpose, your first stop is Seeking and Discovery. This is your realization of yourself and where it all begins. The discovery process requires inner work.

- Your purpose has been showing up in bite-sized portions throughout your life, like clues to a riddle.

- Your path to purpose will require you to assess where you are today and what you envision for your future.

- To discover your purpose, you must identify the life experiences that have been leading you on the path to purpose.

Chapter VI

IDENTIFY YOUR PURPOSE

> *Many plans are in a man's mind, but it is the Lord's purpose for him that will stand. — Proverbs 19:21 Amplified*

To IDENTIFY YOUR PURPOSE, you must first discover and uncover who you are and what gifts you have been blessed with. In the previous chapter, I explained the Seeking and Discovery process and how you can identify your purpose through your life experiences. Now let's discuss your life character traits that have been with you since birth. These traits represent the seeds inside you to be used for your purpose and God's Glory. Of course, these gifts are not new to you; they have been with you for your entire life. What may be new is classifying them as gifts and understanding the role they have in your purpose. Because these traits have been with you for so long, you may not believe that they are significant. For example, if you've been a talker all of your life, you would most likely not identify that as a gift. But do you know that many introverted people have difficulty communicating with others? Instead of hearing "you talk too much" as most talkers are accustomed to hearing, they will most likely hear "speak up" or "stop being so quiet." Have you ever heard the statement, "a closed mouth doesn't get fed?" If you are a talker, you'll most likely never go hungry. If you are blessed to be a talker, and unless you have had the opportunity to speak professionally, you would rarely hear people compliment you for running your mouth, but it is indeed your gift.

Conversely, Introverts are shy, reserved, thoughtful people who do not spend a lot of time talking. They are usually better listeners, and those who are good listeners are generally excellent at strategizing and solving problems. Therefore, it stands to reason that the ability to listen well and speak less is an Introvert's gift. Do you see how this can go both ways? It doesn't matter what side of the spectrum you're on. Both gifts are necessary when appropriately utilized.

To help you with your discovery of purpose, below is a list of seed traits to aid you in identifying the areas in which you excel. This is just a small list to give you a boost of confidence in the right direction. You'll need to put in additional work to continue unlocking your purpose. Highlight the ones that best represent you, and if you don't see any that describe who you are, list your traits on a separate sheet of paper.

Exercise: Character Seed Traits and Discovery

Seed Traits

Talkative	Problem Solver	Leader
Humorous	Counselor	Risk Taker
Sales Leader	Lover of Life	Strong-Willed
Creative	Strategist	Athletic
Musically Inclined	Gifted	Dramatic
Innovator	Caring	Fighter
Organizer	Rebel	Shy
Aggressive	Connector	Easy-Going
Explorer	Intelligent	People-Person

As you look at these traits, can you see how unique your character traits are to who you are? They work so intricately in your design and your purpose on the earth. One of the issues with our society is that our system is set up to fit everyone into a particular box or category, classifying their seed traits as either positive or negative. We see this play out in our world, from the education system to workplaces. Rarely do we celebrate others for their differences. However, it's the differences that make us who we are, and those seed traits qualify us to be more than capable of pursuing our purpose. Always remember everything about your character trait is something God can use for your purpose - even the flaws.

Let me explain this a bit further. My youngest daughter, Winter, is a loud and strong-willed little girl. She is tougher and rougher than most girls her age. As an eight-year-old, her strong personality often gets her into hot water at school and home. She achieves great academic grades, but it's almost a guarantee that we'll see a warning on her conduct card when she comes home from school. In fact, since the age of three, she gave the daycare nursery a run for their money. Was I ecstatic to receive naughty notes from the preschool telling me I had a disorderly child? Of course not! But I have learned over the years that Winter's strong personality isn't going anywhere; it's who she is. As a parent, I can do one of two things. I can try to break her spirit and attempt to control her, and I may achieve some success in the short term because I am her parent, and she is required to listen to me. Or, I can help cultivate her by showing her how to use her 'superpowers' for good - teaching her how to use her voice and strong personality. I can teach her that there is an appropriate time and place to use her voice, and not all situations are conducive to it. I can teach her that she should use her loud voice outdoors and not indoors. I can teach her the right way to use her seed traits. She is loud, bossy, and strong-willed, which indicates that she might be a future leader. She doesn't follow the crowd – that sounds like a game-changer to me. She's not afraid of anything, and it seems like she won't be influenced by others and their way of thinking.

But, how much different would this be for Winter if I compared her to my oldest daughter Kai-Milan? Kai-Milan is the total opposite in her personality. She is a girly girl, who always receives good conduct marks, speaks in turn, and has a soft voice. Kai-Milan lights up a room with her glowing personality; she's the hugger that everyone falls in love with. She doesn't make much of a fuss about things, she's usually non-confrontational, and if the house is too quiet, you can find her curled up in a corner listening to her headphones and watching the latest YouTube science video.

My girls are two different personalities with different seed traits, and I would be doing them a disservice to compare and stifle their uniqueness. Sadly, this happens to too many people, and it delays them from identifying their purpose and understanding their gifts. Instead of being appreciated for their uniqueness, they often find themselves apologizing for simply being themselves. Many seed traits are stifled in their infancy stages because they've existed in environments where people didn't understand that the traits are a blessing and not a curse. Part of the reason many people don't know their purpose is because they have been told over and over that who they are is not fitting.

It's a sad truth that we are often criticized that we are too much of something and not enough of another, and we spend our lives searching for where we fit in. We waste so much of our time trying to fit in a box that someone else made for us. When I shifted my perspective and began to see my seed traits as assets and not liabilities, my net worth immediately increased. I started pursuing the things that I knew I deserved. I moved away from the things that didn't celebrate me, and I learned to accept and acknowledge my responsibility to grow and become, even if people didn't agree or approve of me. God has given me a responsibility to be fruitful and multiply, and I can't allow toxic soil to hinder my growth.

Seed traits were given to each of us, and according to the principle found in the 'Parable of The Talents' in Matthew 25:14-29, we must do our part to multiply them. Now let's look at it from the perspective of the servant who was entrusted with one talent. Can you imagine the thoughts that probably ran through his mind? *Why am I being punished? Didn't I protect the goods? Why is my boss so angry with me?* Think about it. The servant didn't squander, waste, or give away his talent. Actually, he did what he thought was *safe* and kept the talent hidden in a place where no one could tamper with it. However, burying your seed traits is considered disrespectful and dishonorable to our Creator. In the natural, it may seem like a prudent and responsible thing to do, but the act is like a slap in the face of God. He knows who you are, and He knows how He created you. He knows your potential and the impact you will have on this world if you just believe in yourself.

Between Purpose and Responsibility

The traits that formed the foundation of who you are should be valued as positive and not negative attributes. Think about some of your character traits that others have attempted to stop or alter. Granted, there will be some outward displays of traits that you will need to refine as you mature and learn how to be a light in this world, but you should never suppress who God created you to be. Your characteristics and experiences have been preparing you for what your Creator has called you to do. Often, we take our uniqueness for granted because we have become familiar with our traits. I pray that the light bulbs are starting to come on for you. We all have a choice to make when discovering our purpose.

Choice #1: We can put our big girl panties on, do the hard work, and take responsibility for ourselves.

Choice #2: We can whine about where we are, blame everyone else, and stay stuck with no advancement.

Many women find themselves vacillating between choice #1 and choice #2, depending on the day of the week. Being stuck between purpose and responsibility can be a frustrating place. What do you do when God is pulling on you and tugging at you to walk into your purpose, but you have the responsibility of 'adulting?' Life keeps moving, changes keep occurring. Before you know it, ten, fifteen, and even twenty years have passed you by, and you are stuck. I can imagine you asking God, "What do you want me to do? I am doing all that I know how to do. There is no time in my life for Seeking and Discovery. I can barely find five minutes for myself." Trust me, I understand, but you are going to have to fight for this. You are going to have to block out any distraction that keeps you from focusing and tapping in. You must push forward as if your life depends on it.

Please allow me to offer this disclaimer. Pursuing your purpose hardly comes at a convenient time. Life never slows down on its own. In fact, the moment you decide to pursue your purpose, your life will speed up in the form of distractions, including discouragement, doubt, family issues, and the busyness of life. The key is learning to pull away and say 'no' to anything that will not help you arrive at your life's destination. This is where your imaginary life balance scale comes into play. Before you accept another calendar invite or volunteer for another committee, weigh what is essential for you to do right now. There is a way to balance what you need to, and then you must allow God to sort out the rest. You cannot allow the pressure and guilt from others to limit you from moving forward in purpose.

I remembered praying to become a better wife and mother. I felt I was failing miserably at both because I wanted to do it all, but I knew I was neglecting my family. I wanted to have a successful business, have family dinners, go out on weekly dates, have family nights with the kids, and find time for myself. I couldn't do it all at the same time. Often, I would feel guilty about spending less time with my family and not having my children involved in extracurricular activities. After I decided to work my business full-time, we began to experience the growing pains first-hand. My husband wasn't always on board. There were many disagreements about how my purpose fit in with the family's vision. Thankfully after a few adjustments, we learned how to work together as a family and team. Truthfully, I was out of balance trying to do it all. I had too much on my plate. I had to learn how to identify my season and adjust my 'to-do list and priorities accordingly. Any offer that didn't align with my season and purpose received a big fat "no." Ecclesiastes 3 teaches us that there is a season for everything in this life, a time to plant and a time to reap. Learning about the seasons of life helped me to focus more and navigate successfully towards my calling. The refocus created a stress-free life that resulted in a peaceful home environment. We created a family vision that incorporated both of our individual life pursuits. This helped us to raise our children in a healthy and nurturing environment, the way God intended.

A toxic home environment is not conducive to pursuing purpose. A cluttered mind and life are the enemies of purpose, and this is where it gets tricky for women. By nature, we are nurturers which equates to us serving everyone first and ourselves last. What I am telling you to do probably goes against everything in the fiber of your being. But it's necessary and good for you. It's time for you to become selfish with your time and personal space. It's time for you to put yourself in priority space #1. It's time for you to be intentional about who you spend your time talking to and how you schedule your day. I won't go too deep into this, but one of the exercises I have clients complete is to keep a detailed account of their day for five days, including everything from the time they wake up to the time they go to sleep. This includes all projects and various activities to tracking the time spent on phone calls and even their time commuting. They often notice that there is so much time wasted throughout their day. They also clearly identify the energy and time suckers that need to be addressed and adjusted. When they tell me they don't have the time, I show them that they do; they're just not using it wisely. The foundation of Purpose 101 is creating the time to focus and understand your path to purpose. This will require you to restructure the way you've been doing things.

Identify Your Purpose

Journaling has been an effective tool in helping me sort out the experiences that led me to discover purpose. It has been so transformative that I have introduced this process to every client I work with to help them unlock memories, key life details and bring the layers of their story together. When I was younger, we wrote our feelings down into a diary. Diaries are old-school mini-journals with a lock and key that kept young girls' most sincere and intimate thoughts. We considered them to be a rite of passage. I had a lavender one with a small gold lock and key. Every night before bed, I would write in my little diary. It contained my innermost secrets, things that I didn't want to talk about with anyone else. It helped me put my true feelings and experiences into words. As I became older, I forgot all about my diary. Sometimes we forget about the little things we used to do as a kid that helped us. As an adult, I graduated from writing in a diary to writing my thoughts in a journal.

When working with my clients, I give them the assignment to journal their thoughts for thirty days. During the thirty days, they are instructed to spend quiet time asking God to reveal who they are. I want to encourage you to do this as well. You may ask the question, *"what will journaling for the next 30 days do for me?"* It will allow you to write down the feelings, thoughts, and emotions that you don't talk about. You may be wondering how this helps connect you to your purpose. Throughout this book, I have been talking to you about knowing what you are carrying. To answer this, you'll not only need to go through your discovery process, but you'll need to process your experiences and how they shaped you into the person you are today. You'll need to go deep into your story and uncover the making of who you are. It will all start to come together and lead you to your purpose. Journaling will help you unclog the drain in your mind, and it is a form of brain dumping. Your mind is filled with so many things in life that most times, it's hard for you to see your way clearly. By journaling, you can connect the dots that lead you to purpose. Personally, journaling helps me to stay in alignment with my thoughts and feelings. It's probably not new to you, so this may be a refresher or reminder to keep you focused. The process may seem overwhelming at first, especially when you take your trip down memory lane, but by doing the inner work, you'll find it much easier to reach your destination.

In your journal, write everything, and I mean everything that you feel. You'll write about old memories and situations. You'll write about the amazing woman you are, filled with unique talents and capabilities. You'll write out your "I am Thankful" list. You'll write your affirmations. You'll write scriptures that minister to where you are right now. In addition to your thoughts and feelings, I want you to take some time to reflect on what the people in your life (parents, guardians, grandparents, older siblings, teachers) have said about your personality. What did they notice about you? Can you see these traits as positive contributions to your purpose? Think about these things as you began to understand your purpose. Write these reflections in your journal. Take some time to sit in this moment. This should start to feel like a breath of fresh air. This is the beginning of identifying and acknowledging your purpose. Remember what I mentioned to you earlier - God doesn't reveal your purpose to you all at once. The more you walk down the road, the clearer the signs will become.

> **But when he, the Spirit of truth, comes, he will guide you into all the truth. – John 16:13**

Let's keep building on your discovery from the last few chapters and use those clues to clearly identify and articulate your purpose. Up until now, we have talked about the Seeking and Discovery process. There is a difference between knowing you may have a purpose and being so sure that you have a purpose that you won't stop until you discover and live it. I pray by now that you are in alignment with the latter.

> *"The purpose of life is to be useful, to be honorable, to be compassionate, to have it make some difference that you have lived and lived well."* – Ralph Waldo Emerson

As you are starting to identify your purpose, if you are not careful, you will find yourself fearful of putting a label on it. As humans, we inherently have a fear of choosing the wrong path for our life. I've heard it said that women are the most indecisive beings. We have plans A, B, C, AA, BB, and CC – just in case. We have a backup plan to our backup plan. I believe we do this as a safety blanket to protect ourselves from life's disappointments. However, when you are ready to identify your purpose, this is the one time when it's acceptable not to have a backup plan. This is where you must trust that God has been revealing the clues to you all along. This is not the time to fear. This is not the time to doubt or have a lack of belief in yourself or your abilities. I am not promising that you'll hit it precisely the first time. However, you can be comforted in knowing there is room for error – you're human. Although it's my prayer that this book will help you to identify your purpose, you may need to take more time to unlock it. I want you to review everything we have discussed in the last few chapters, as well as your responses. At this point, there should be some bells ringing in your ear. You have identified what your seed traits are. You have identified your life experiences and the lessons you have learned from them. Take a look at your answers and start journaling your thoughts about what you have written. You are now ready to begin identifying your purpose.

Purpose Clarity Exercise I:

Think about your life experiences and the character seed traits you have utilized along the way and answer the sentences below. Fill in the blank as it best describes you.

I know that I am great at (think about the thing(s) that people are constantly calling on you to do).

_____

_____

_____

I am passionate about bringing hope, healing and restoration to _____ because _____

_____

_____

_____

What are some things I can do to bring betterment to this world? _____

_____

_____

_____

I have always had dreams about doing _____

_____

_____

_____

When I am _____
(activity) I feel alive and free.

I feel God most when I am _____

_____

_____

Continue with the questions below. Read them out loud, and then write down the visualizations and thoughts that come to your mind. Stay in this moment as long as you need to. Close your eyes and meditate on what you feel and see.

> God, what is my purpose?
> Who have you called me to be?
> Why did You choose me?

As you ask these questions, you may be flooded with thoughts and emotions. This is exactly where you need to be. The thoughts and feelings you are having at this moment are God's reassurance to you. Write everything you hear or feel in your spirit down in your journal. Don't be overwhelmed by the rush of emotion. You will make this journey, one step at a time.

Are things starting to become more clearer to you? Clearly answering those questions is vital because your purpose is more than just fulfilling your personal goals. Your purpose is bigger than your current influence. Your purpose serves a cause and a world much bigger than you. Your purpose will affect and impact the lives of others. Let's take this a step further. I want you to write and declare your purpose vision statement below. I have included mine from the previous chapter to give you a glimpse into what this should look like. Your purpose statement should consist of the who, what, why, and how.

Vision Statement

My purpose is to help change the lives of 1,000,000 women around the world. I will help them find their purpose and unlock their voices through my writings, business coaching, life coaching, family counseling, and professional speaking.

Complete your purpose vision statement below.

My purpose is to _____

_____

_____

_____

_____

Does it feel good to start identifying your true self? This should be a breakthrough for you to create a pathway to allow you to be free and open to accept yourself as a gift to the world. You have just walked through your purpose clarity exercises and have put together your purpose vision statement. These are the components of identifying your purpose. If you still have blockages and feel stuck, go back to the exercises and meditate deeply on them. Remember, identifying your purpose is simply identifying the thing or things you have been placed on this earth to do that will leave a lasting impact on those around you and beyond. Between Seeking and Discovery and identifying your purpose is the gray area called processing. If you find yourself there, you are not excluded from doing the work. You are expected to put a demand on purpose by forming your words and speaking daily affirmations to create an atmosphere for birthing purpose. If you need a spiritual boost, declare the below declaration out loud in front of the mirror.

> **Today I am walking in my purpose. God has positioned me in the right place at the right time, and He is revealing to me His purpose for my life. My spirit is in agreement and ready to hear and receive.**

How Will I Know?

The million-dollar question is often asked, "How will I know when I've found purpose?" I can answer this based on my personal experience. When I found my purpose, it felt like my life had meaning. I started to become a woman that made an impact and changed people's lives. People began to thank me through their words and compliments. I discovered that my purpose was to impact the lives of people. The path that I had already traveled throughout my life had prepared me for my purpose. But truthfully, the path was difficult. I didn't have anyone who took me by the hand and showed me how to get to where I am today. My mentors and role models could only lead me to the furthest point they had experienced in their own lives. I am blessed that I didn't stay stuck at those deliberating crossroads. I am grateful that I identified my purpose and began to build myself up. The experiences were all stepping stones that were necessary for my journey. I mentioned previously that my family moved to Houston without much of anything. Had I looked at what I saw with my natural eyes, I would have missed my purpose and moved back to Florida, where it was comfortable, convenient and where I had my family and support team. This would have felt good to my flesh, but my spirit would have been out of alignment. I had to tap into my relationship with God to help me understand that new territory and become active in moving my life forward.

There was a difference in my life when I discovered purpose. I became a genuinely happy person from the inside out. The bouts of depression I previously battled with disappeared. New doors of opportunities became available, and I always seemed to be in the right place at the right time. When I submitted to my purpose, I released the responsibility of making sure everything in my life was perfect, and I learned how to trust and lean on my Heavenly Father for everything. My relationships became more genuine, and I felt good about the impact I was making with others. Everything felt new. There was an inner fulfillment, and I wanted to share how I felt with others.

Positivity is contagious. My life became more goal-driven and focused, and I had little time for procrastination and distractions. I became unapologetic and bold as I released my feelings of shame and guilt. I started to see life from a new perspective. One of my favorite scriptures growing up was Romans 8:28, "And we know that all things work together for the good of those that love God and are called according to His purpose by Christ Jesus." At such a young age, I had no concept of what that scripture meant. I didn't know why I liked it, but now I know why I was drawn to it. It all makes sense now. Everything from our past all works together for our good. This consists of the good, the ugly, and the memories we want to forget. They all lead us to our destiny.

> *"No one bumps into purpose; you must actively pursue it. Purpose takes action, focus, and determination to prepare for where you're going. It doesn't drop in your lap; you have to be actively engaged in the pursuit of it."* —Dr. Sherrie Walton

Chapter VI Recap

- The traits that are the foundation of who you are should be valued as positive and not negative.

- As you are starting to identify your purpose, if you are not careful, you will find yourself fearful of putting a label on it.

- Journaling will help you unclog the drain in your mind and is a form of brain dumping. Your mind is filled with so many things in life that most times, it's hard for you to see your way clearly. By journaling, you can connect the dots that lead you to purpose.

- Identifying your purpose is simply understanding what you have been placed on this earth to do to leave a lasting impact on those around you and beyond.

- No one bumps into purpose; you must actively pursue it.

Chapter VII

BIRTHING PURPOSE

> *For the vision is yet for an appointed time, but at the end, it shall speak, and not lie: though it tarry, wait for it; because it will surely come, it will not tarry.* – Habakkuk 2:3

THERE IS EXCITEMENT IN the air when an expectant mother announces she's having a baby. It's a common practice for her to receive a response with the question, "what are you having?" We all want to know. I feel this same excitement when a woman recognizes she can define and articulate her purpose. When she does, she suddenly becomes inundated with an inner glow, a light that shines and shifts how she sees the world. A woman who discovers her purpose walks with a look of determination and evokes a level of confidence that cannot be explained.

As you continue on the quest, you will discover that your purpose will be manifested in stages. This chapter will help you understand how to process this new revelation and know where you may be right now and how to move forward with the proper strategy. It's not surprising that the thought of your purpose may cause you to feel overwhelmed or even intimidated. It's not uncommon to ask yourself, *'How in the world am I supposed to accomplish this vision with limited time and resources?'* Rest assured that you are not expected to fulfill or fund the vision all at once. You'll move forward in purpose, in bite-sized pieces, processing what you can on the level of where you are. For example, if you know your purpose will lead you to the nations of the world to speak and uplift others, your first duty will be to talk to those in your home, then your community, then your state, and so on. Your purpose journey is just like attending school; you will enroll in courses that apply to your level of comprehension. Once you have successfully passed the coursework, you'll graduate to the next level. Your ability to grasp the necessary lesson and apply what you've learned will qualify you for your promotion.

You are not responsible for manifesting your purpose. This is God's responsibility. You are responsible for carrying out the vision by doing the work and becoming better, wiser, and stronger in your assignment. You are the steward and not the owner. Trying to take control of our lives is where many of us run into trouble. We are such big dreamers and overachievers that we often attempt to figure out the how and why of the big picture, while the smaller steps are often seen as insignificant.

I had a revelation about this very thing in my own life. While in prayer about the expansion of my business, the Holy Spirit revealed the required submission to the season of life that I was in. While it's clear my vision is to impact the world, the foundation of this vision is good stewardship over the people that He has given me responsibility for – my children. They are the first manifestation of the seed I am sowing into the world; they are my harvest. As I am moving in my day-to-day of coaching others and encouraging them to walk in their purpose, I must not neglect the first assignment of my purpose. My responsibility as a parent is much more than just making sure my children's physical needs are met and providing them with a solid education. It's about the quality time I spend with them to help cultivate their gifts and purpose by personally listening and teaching them solid lessons that will carry them throughout their lives. Their exposure to spiritual and life principles directly reflects how well I teach and coach them.

Often, we like to skip over our primary responsibilities because they don't come with accolades and notes of appreciation. However, until we master what's done in the dark – without the lights and cameras, we won't be ready to handle the platforms that are awaiting us. What if more of us had this revelation about the stage or season we are in, as it relates to birthing purpose? This would certainly help eliminate the unnecessary frustrations, impatience, and feelings we have while in pursuit. It will take away the doubts and worries that tell us that life isn't moving fast enough. Think about this. How irrational is it for a mother in her first trimester to complain about having to wait through two more additional trimesters before the baby is ready to be birthed? Of course, she could complain, but would it do her any good? Would her complaining shorten the time that it takes to develop a healthy baby? This is why the doctor explains the expectations of the birthing trimesters.

As we move further into the discussion of birthing purpose, we'll analyze the three stages of birthing purpose parallel to the natural childbirth experience. When a woman is pregnant, her physical body must align with the process of giving birth. The necessary body parts and organs adjust to accommodate the birthing at the end of nine months. It's amazing how our Creator fashioned our bodies to be strong enough to give birth naturally – almost without much work needed on our part. As our baby grows inside us, our body naturally adapts and provides the baby with the nutrients required to live and survive in the world after it has exited the birth canal. The woman's body during childbirth is such a miraculous thing. Our part in carrying the baby is to understand its birthing process and do our part of eating healthy and providing a safe internal and external environment, as best we can, to aid in its growth and development. Now think about this as it relates to the birthing of purpose. There are conditions you must meet to prepare to walk in your calling. Positioning yourself through the right associations and conversations is imperative. Understanding that you are the most essential person in this process is also necessary. You need to understand your worth. In the labor and delivery room, you are the only one pregnant and giving birth. As I have said before, you are already equipped with everything you need to birth your purpose.

As your physical body works to produce the baby, your spirit man works hand in hand to prepare you for giving birth. I have stressed throughout this book how critical your spiritual walk is. To birth purpose, your spirit must be strong enough to endure the process. This is an essential foundational piece to birthing a healthy purpose. You must begin as a healthy person – mind, body, and soul. Think about the physical endurance that is required when your natural body must prepare to birth your baby. Knowing what to expect during the process will help you to be ready as you give birth. This, in turn, will allow you to have a balanced perspective to grow and cultivate your gifts. Throughout our purpose journey, we have unlocked your traits, characteristics, and experiences that have positioned you to give birth. Just like your natural birthing process, you need to understand what trimester you are in right now. Assessing where you are will help you to make the best decisions for your season.

The Three Stages of Birthing Purpose

The first trimester of birthing your purpose includes Seeking and Discovery. By now, you should be entirely comfortable with this stage, as we discussed this extensively in the previous chapters. Just a quick recap, this is the stage where you ask questions like, *Who am I?* and *Why am I here?* This is the stage where you acknowledge something is taking place in your life, even though you can't quite put a label on it. You know things are shifting, and your appetite for people and places is quickly changing. During this first trimester of pregnancy, you begin to identify the things that make you uneasy. You feel a shift in your life and your perspective. This is the time when you start to understand yourself. In Seeking and Discovery, you recollect and address old memories and experiences. You analyze people, circumstances, decisions you've made, and relationships you've had. This can be a difficult stage because it causes you to face memories of your past and address any areas that require you to forgive and grow. This is where you cut soul-ties and allow yourself time to heal and bloom. The beautiful side of Seeking and Discovery is that you put aside the ideas and plans that others once influenced you with, and you find parts of your inner self that have been buried away. This is your freedom stage.

Now just because you are pregnant doesn't mean it's time to shout it from the rooftops. Even in your excitement, you need to remain quiet. My husband and I had the privilege of officiating a wedding of an amazing couple who we have grown to love. Not too long after their marriage, they announced to us they were expecting. We were overjoyed to hear the news; they really wanted to have a child after losing their first baby, and I knew this was God's way of showing them that He hadn't forgotten about them. As excited as I was for them and knowing how anxious they would be to share the news, I immediately advised the expectant mommy not to mention her pregnancy outside of her immediate family until she had completed her first trimester. I remember when my mom gave me the same advice. I never questioned her because I assumed she knew what she was talking about. But quite honestly, I never knew outside of my immediate circle it was a thing to do until I began to write this book. I kept my pregnancy quiet because that's what my mom told me to do. I never questioned why she told me to do it. I just assumed it was to keep the nosey people and gossip circles from out of my business. Now I know it was more than that, with a slight inclusion of the latter.

As I was writing this book, I began to do my own research on the topic. Interestingly, I discovered many reasons to keep quiet about your pregnancy during its infancy stages, and it wasn't just some old wives' tale passed on from generation to generation. There were women around the world from Australia to Canada chiming in on the topic. According to the University of California San Francisco, "the first trimester is the most crucial to your baby's development.[1] During this period, your baby's body structure and organ systems develop. Most miscarriages and birth defects occur during this period. Your body also undergoes significant changes during the first trimester."[1] This explains why women are generally moody and face so much uncertainty during this time. I believe this is true while carrying our purpose as well.

---

1   University of California San Francisco/ https://www.ucsfhealth.org/conditions/pregnancy/trimesters (Accessed 01/01/2021)

The beginning or first trimester of any pregnancy is the most critical time. This is the time when you should sit still and allow God to minister to you. Don't assume that you know what you're doing, as this is new territory. Your focus is to carry your purpose to full-term, with no threats or complications. Consult with your Creator about this new 'thing' you're carrying.

The second trimester of birthing purpose includes Vision Planning, Acceptance, and Preparation. Now that you have identified your purpose, you can begin to see the vision and begin to understand how this may look in your future. During your **Vision Planning,** you will have the ability to plan your future according to the revelation revealed by the Holy Spirit. Don't limit your vision. Dream as big as you possibly can. Also, keep in mind your purpose is not for selfish gain and fulfillment. Anything in your vision that makes you want to serve yourself more than you want to help others is out of alignment.

During the Vision Planning, you should 'identify your why.' We hear this phrase quite often from motivational speakers and life coaches. This isn't just hype. Your 'why' is the reason you do what you do. Identifying your 'why' is essential because it's a constant reminder that keeps you moving forward when you want to throw in the towel. Your 'why' helps you stay connected to your purpose and provides an emotional attachment. As you pursue your vision, you'll realize that it's less about the activity and more about the passion behind what you do. This is what keeps people serving in their capacities and evolving into world changers. My personal 'why' is to create a legacy for my children and generations that will follow according to Proverbs 13:22, "A good man (woman) leaves an inheritance to his/her children's children." This 'why' drives me to keep going. If you haven't done so already, take a moment to identify your 'why.'

Your Vision Planning will answer why, what, who, when, and how.

> ***Why*** are you passionate about your purpose/cause? *Why* do you want to bring change to that area?
>
> ***What*** problem will your purpose solve? *What* can you do to bring about change?
>
> ***Who*** is the demographic your purpose will help? *Who* needs the solution you have?
>
> ***How*** will you carry out your purpose?
>
> ***When*** will you begin walking in your purpose?

After Vision Planning, you enter the Acceptance stage. During this stage, you accept what you have learned about yourself and apply it to your vision. During the Acceptance stage, you will receive your validation from God *only*. You do not need to concern yourself with the opinions of others. During Acceptance, you acknowledge and appreciate your characteristics and personality traits. This is when you accept yourself without any apologies and become thankful for your life because now you know why you are the way you are. This is the celebration of yourself. One key to fulfilling your purpose is accepting who you are, no matter how intimidating to others it may be.

The Preparation Stage is next. Let me warn you, in this new excitement and revelation, be very careful not to move forward without first having the strategy. This is where many people lose. Not being adequately prepared will produce poor results. It doesn't matter how anointed you are or how good your gifts are; you'll inevitably face burnout, discouragement, and defeat without adequate preparation (spiritually, emotionally, physically). Do not rush through this phase. This is your time to make plans and line up the pieces.

The third trimester includes Birthing and Activation. This is where you will put action to the vision. As you passed through each stage, you gained more knowledge and wisdom on who you are and why God chose you for the journey. You can go ahead and breathe now. You have worked through many of the kinks of your pregnancy. You have not only accepted that you are pregnant, but you are ready to give birth. Your Birthing and Activation stage is where you will experience most of your trial and errors, don't let this stop you. In fact, you should push harder.

Let me explain how Birthing and Activation translates into manifestation. If you have been called to birth a ministry, the Birthing and Activation is the first day of service. If you have been called to start a Nonprofit Organization, the Birthing and Activation is enrolling your first client. If you have been called to start a business, the Birthing and Activation is your first paid customer. I want to specify this because some will confuse the act of doing the research, ordering the business card, or telling others about what your plans are as the Activation. No, ma'am, that's not Birthing and Activation. Birthing comes with pain. There is pain when you establish a new organization and put in the sweat equity. There is pain when you are not supported by those you expected to be there. There is pain when you encounter those you thought wanted to help you, but they really wanted to steal your ideas and copy your infrastructure. Don't confuse the planning process with the Activation process.

You're in Labor

When I was pregnant with my son, the excitement of pregnancy had worn off as I approached my 42nd week of pregnancy. Yes, you read that correctly – 42 weeks. It was the summertime, I was miserable, and Miami's heat was brutal. I arrived at my doctor's appointment for my weekly checkup and was disappointed when he told me the baby had only dilated one centimeter, the same as my last visit the week before. It was apparent that my son had no plans to exit the womb and make his grand appearance anytime soon. Frustrated, I explained to my gynecologist that I had been doing everything he had instructed me to make the baby drop. Walking at the mall, squats, and even sex – but nothing had changed. "Is there anything we can do?" I asked desperately. The doctor suggested labor induction, and immediately my heart dropped. This was not good news for me. I wanted to have a natural childbirth without any assistance from modern medicine, but I also knew I needed to do what was best for the baby. My husband and I headed back to our home to pick up my overnight bag, eat a small meal, and prepare to meet our new son.

When I checked into the hospital, they escorted me to the birthing room, changed me out of my clothes, and strapped me up to the monitors. I declined to have the epidural, despite being nearly harassed by the nurse to take it. She insisted it was needed to avoid the pain she said would be forthcoming. I silently dismissed her words while praying underneath my breath. For my entire pregnancy, I prayed for a painless child birthing experience. I put my faith in those words. My philosophy has always been that women have been having babies for ages before modern medicine, and I believe my body would perform up to the way it was created.

PUSH!

What you experience through your birthing process is entirely up to you. Having the right mindset and preparation is critical. A toxic mindset is a sure sign you're not mature enough to birth your purpose. The proper mindset is also important so you won't self-sabotage and limit yourself. When I was pregnant, a friend gave me a copy of a book entitled "Supernatural Childbirth" by Janice Mize. That book taught me how to pray and create an expectancy for a healthy, thriving baby. I daily prayed over my child while he was in my womb and thanked God for the gift He had given me. I also declared that I would not experience the pains of childbirth and that I would have a quick and easy delivery. Now I know that may seem crazy to some people, and I am okay with that, but I can honestly say that my expectations were exactly what I experienced. I heard other women screaming from their birthing rooms; some had been in delivery for over 24 hours while others had to have emergency c-sections. There's a vivid memory of that experience I applied to my birthing experience. My mom came into the room and dropped a nugget I used as a secret weapon that hurried my delivery process. She told me every time I felt a contraction – push. She had done it during her five natural childbirth deliveries, and she had a proven track record of popping out her babies and bouncing back. She had street-cred with me. I did it. Every time my cervix contracted, I pushed. This went on for almost six hours until I heard the doctor say, "stop pushing; the baby is here!"

If you had a terrible childbirth experience, this is not an insult to you in any way. This is simply to point out that our experiences can be shaped by what we believe. I applied the techniques in that book for my second and third child, and each birth became easier and easier, with the last baby being delivered in under 45 minutes. What are you saying, Sherrie? I am saying that I want you to allow God to create personal experiences with you and not base your life on what others have experienced.

The Birthing Room

The delivery of your purpose is where you will experience the most pain. To move your purpose from the inside to the outside, you must endure during the birthing experience. You need to push. The birthing process involves taking the necessary actions required. The birthing process is where you do the thing that you have been called or predestined to do. In other words, this is not the time where you are trying out theories or doing your research, or going to school. The birthing process is your 'go' time. It's also the time when you will experience the most pain. Remember my story about giving birth to my Mommy and Me Conference in Dallas? I alluded to how difficult this was for me and how I had to choose birthing purpose over attending my grandmother's funeral. That's what the birthing room feels like. You'll have tears, misunderstandings, and lonely times. It's all a part of the process. When I was in labor with my son, instead of concentrating on the pain, I chose to think about how amazing it was to be giving birth to a human being. I envisioned what he would look like and how I was going to feel as I held him. I counted my experience as a blessing, and I was thankful that I would deliver a beautiful, healthy boy.

As you transition into your purpose:

1. Set your mind on what is working and not what isn't.
2. Create an atmosphere conducive to birthing purpose.
3. Follow the instructions of the doctor (Holy Spirit).
4. Build up your endurance before you enter the delivery room.
5. Nurture your purpose.
6. PUSH!

Birthing your purpose means you must do the work. It's your calling and your responsibility. It's time to push and breathe.

Chapter VII Recap

- You will move forward in purpose, in bite-sized pieces, processing what you can on the level of where you are.

- Your purpose journey is just like attending school; you will enroll in courses that apply to your level of comprehension. Once you successfully pass the coursework, you will graduate to the next level. Your ability to grasp the necessary lesson and apply what you have learned will qualify you for your promotion.

- You are not responsible for manifesting your purpose. This is God's responsibility.

- There are three trimesters in birthing purpose.
    - Trimester One: Seeking and Discovery
    - Trimester Two: Vision Planning, Acceptance and Preparation
    - Trimester Three: Birthing and Activation

- The delivery of your purpose is where you will experience the most pain. To move your purpose from the inside to the outside, you must endure through the birthing experience. You need to push!

Chapter VIII

YOUR BIG ANNOUNCEMENT

> *There is a time for everything and a season for every activity under the heavens. – Ecclesiastes 3:1 NIV*

AFTER YOU HAVE DISCOVERED your purpose, in your excitement, you will want to tell everyone – wait – don't it! Maybe, not so soon, at least. Eventually, everyone will be able to see your results in due time, so don't be so quick to run and tell – just yet. I am not swearing you into the CIA or a special operative unit. I am just advising you to wait until you have everything in alignment. It's not easy when you are walking the purpose journey alone. Trust me, I understand, but it's in your best interest to be silent while God does His work in you. I founded an organization that supports women in their efforts to birth purpose. It was created to provide a safe place for like-minded women to unite and help each other build, grow, and flourish to become the women they have been called to be.

> *Those who guard their lips preserve their lives, but those who speak rashly will come to ruin. – Proverbs 13:3*

You need to protect your gift until it is the right time to share it. Keeping it private helps to delay any negativity and personal opinions that are bound to come your way. It's not always wise to share news about what you're doing until you know it's the right time to go public. There is a time and a place to be silent and a time to speak, according to Ecclesiastes 3:7. When starting in business almost eighteen years ago, my mentors encouraged me to stay quiet and move in silence until the deal was closed and the bag was secured. It wasn't fear; it was wisdom. Speaking too soon may have cost me the deal or allowed one of my competitors to slip in and undermine me. This was before the days of social media, and this concept goes against everything that we see today. It's very seldom that you log into your social media account without seeing every single detail about someone's life plastered on your timeline – from what they ate to the state of their relationships. We live in a culture where you are encouraged to expose everything about your life to connect with others and gain their approval. The danger in this is that words have power. And no matter how spiritual you may be, the last thing you want to do is to spend your time warring against the negative words others have spoken over you. The weapons may not prosper, but why give them a chance to form?

Do you remember the story of Joseph, the son of Jacob, in the Bible? Well, if not, let me give you the short version. He was a dreamer, and he was favored by his father, Jacob. His father gave him a coat of many colors, and he didn't give one to the other brothers. It was a custom gift; it was made just for him. Joseph began having dreams, and in his dreams, his family was bowing down to him. The brothers, of course, didn't like this and decided to punish him and shut him up. They handled the situation by throwing him into a ditch, ripping his coat into pieces, and selling him off into slavery. Had Joseph been a friend of mine, I would have encouraged him to keep quiet about his dream until God had shown him the strategy or even the next step. Now, that doesn't alleviate those that would have been jealous of him in the first place, but I believe he would not have had to suffer as much as he did.

The key concepts I pulled from Joseph's story was:

- The people closest to you can be the very ones that shut you down.
- Be careful that someone disguised as a 'brother' or 'sister' isn't the one that has been planted to take you out.
- Speaking too soon can cause a detour or delay to your purpose.
- You may not see it, but there are people in your inner circle that will be jealous of your gift.

- The vision you see will need time to fully manifest. It may not be for right now.
- When God gives you a glimpse into your future – approach it with humility.
- You must understand your purpose before you try and share it with others.
- Shut your mouth!

Joseph interpreted his dream to mean that his brothers would bow down to him. Remember when I mentioned that your purpose serves a mission bigger than you? Had Joseph known this, he could have responded differently. He may have interpreted his dream as an opportunity for position and power over his brothers. However, God's plan was to align Joseph to be the vessel to save his family. His family needed him to be in the position of power that he was later promoted to in Pharaoh's kingdom. Eventually, his dream did come to pass at the right time, and he saved his family. However, he may have had a better experience had he stayed silent and let God work it out for him instead of talking too much and too soon.

You Don't Need Validation

Before you share the details of your calling with anyone, check your motives as to why you may be anxious to share your news. Make sure you're wanting to share the information from a genuine place, and not just to prove your haters wrong. If we're not careful, we can be a bit petty inside when we start to see the table of success prepared before our enemies. Validation is not a prerequisite for success; it's quite the opposite. Besides, when you give birth, you'll be too busy to pay attention or be concerned about the accolades of others. Ask any new mother if she has much time for anything else outside of taking care of her new baby. As a reminder, you do not need validation from others. We have all agreed that fulfilling purpose isn't about anyone else but you, so technically, you never need to announce it. When you walk in your purpose, it will reveal itself. The light will shine so brightly from you that no one will be able to deny you are a woman fulfilling purpose.

> *You are the light of the world. A city that is set on a hill cannot be hidden. – Matthew 5:14 NKJV.*

Too much acceptance can be a disaster for failure. Be careful when too many people are cheering you on. Those with the right mindset will be generally happy for you. Before you make any significant announcements about your moves, pray about it. You want to be sure that you don't make any premature moves that can result in casualties. There may not be another opportunity for you, and I am not saying this to frighten you, but I want you to know the importance of moving too soon. The Bible tells us to pray without ceasing. Because our Heavenly Father has a clear view of the chessboard, He knows when and how you should make a move and when to move the King, Queen, Bishop, or Knight. For those who don't play chess, it may be a good time for you to study a little about the game.

Pursuing your purpose will allow you to see those who have your best interest at heart. It will also reveal those hanging around you because of the value you bring. Purpose killers and energy suckers are more concerned about getting more out of you than they are willing to offer. Avoid them at all costs and if they try to give you advice at any time, take it with a grain of salt.

Have you met any **"Purpose Killers"** before? Allow me to introduce you to them.

Conceited Cindy- This is the person that makes every conversation about her. Talking to her is exhausting. When you tell her what you have accomplished, she tells you that she's done more.

Doubting Debra- This is the person that doubts everything. She doesn't believe it will work until she sees it, and even then, she doubts it is true. Because she is afraid to step out in her own life, she talks down on everyone's dream.

Faithless Faith- This is the super religious friend that knows every scripture for your life but always has a problem applying the same word to her own life. She is waiting on God to move (so she says), and her life hasn't improved in the past ten years.

Gossiping Gina- This person always has the community news or the "tea" on everyone. She always keeps you informed. You know she spreads your business as quickly as you hang up the phone.

Negative Nancy- This is the person that never has anything positive to say. She is a miserable complainer, and she makes sure everyone around her is miserable. It's always a cloudy day; things are always bleak.

Prideful Patty- This is the one who thinks that she can do what you do better than you. And instead of working with you, she competes against you.

Super-Critical Susan- This is the person that is critical of everything anyone does. Although constructive criticism can be helpful, criticizing your ideas and their implementation without justification will cause an issue.

Talkative Tanya- This person always has advice on how you should live your life and never lets you get in a word. She constantly interrupts and talks over you. At the end of your conversation, you often wonder if she heard anything you had to say.

Vindictive Vickie- This is the person that has been waiting for the right moment to bring you down. She knows enough about you to destroy your reputation. She constantly reminds you of everything she's done for you – you owe her.

After reading the above list, you may be wondering who you can trust that would be sensitive to your announcement.

One of my favorite sayings is 'go where you're celebrated and not where you're tolerated.' The same applies to your purpose. There is a safe place around like-minded, purpose-driven people that will help you cultivate your gift. One of your prayers should be for God to direct you to your destiny helpers, the people positioned to help you fulfill your destiny. These people will acknowledge your gifts and value, are equipped with the resources, and are willing to help you. Also, know that resources are not always monetary. Resources can be connections, knowledge, skillsets, favor, and doors of opportunity.

As a warning, keep your purpose away from the opinions of others. People will come around you, and they will provide their views about what they feel you should do and how you should do it. Although we respect those who believe in us, make sure their opinion does not override what you know you should be doing. Their views of your purpose will be limited by their experiences with you. For example, if you wanted to start a business and never had one before, people around you will most likely tell you that it's something that you should be extremely cautious about. They'll say to you, maybe you shouldn't leave your good job, or perhaps you shouldn't step out on faith. There will always be some risks when pursuing your purpose, and most people are not comfortable taking risks. If you talk to someone who does not usually take risks in their lives, they generally won't be able to see the vision that God has given you. The Bible talks about having wise counsel, but I believe wise counsel will guide you in the areas in which they have the expertise. In other words, if you are taking counsel from someone who has never accomplished what you are seeking to achieve, then I don't believe that's seeking wise counsel. The Holy Spirit is there to guide you on what you should do.

When Should You Make the Announcement?

Before you make any announcements, you want to ensure that you are equipped and ready to move forward. For example, if you are considering leaving your workplace to pursue your purpose, you probably should hold off on telling everyone in your department until you are ready to put in your notice. If you are considering opening a business, the best time to announce it would be after incorporating the company and not when you have the concept only. You don't need to rush it. If you think about the birth analogy we have been using throughout this book, a good time would be after you have given birth – or at the earliest, after the first trimester. When the time is right, you'll know it. It will come up in an organic conversation – it won't be forced and won't come across as if you are bragging.

Trust me, you won't need to keep silent the entire time; just make sure you have a support system to help you. There are people that you can share your joy. Now I say this cautiously, but I must say it because I have found it to be accurate more times than not. Those that are happiest for you may not be those that are the closest to you. Sometimes you'll find perfect strangers who will be more excited and ready to celebrate with you and hold your hand during the journey. My suggestion is to wait until you are out of your danger zone. This is after you're out of the planning stages and in full execution mode. When the time is right, you won't be concerned with the opinions of others, and you'll be secure in who you are and who you have been called to be. Before you make the big announcement, wait until you have clear direction from the Holy Spirit to make sure you're ready to go.

Chapter VIII Recap

- You must protect your purpose until it is the right time to share it. Keeping it private helps to delay any negativity and personal opinions that are bound to come your way.

- Make sure your motive is to share the news from a genuine place and not just to prove your haters wrong.

- Pursuing your purpose will allow you to see those who have your best interest at heart. It will also reveal those hanging around you only because of the value you bring to them.

- Before you make any announcements, you want to ensure you are equipped and ready to move forward.

- Those that are happiest for you may not be those that are the closest to you. Sometimes, you'll find perfect strangers who will be more excited and ready to celebrate with you and hold your hand during the journey.

Chapter IX

YOUR NEW JOURNEY

> *God blessed them and said to them, "Be fruitful and increase in number; fill the earth and subdue it. Rule over the fish in the sea and the birds in the sky and over every living creature that moves on the ground. – Genesis 1:28, NIV*

AFTER GIVING BIRTH TO my purpose, there was an immediate fear that overtook me. The best way to describe it was a feeling of inadequacy – not feeling as if I was good enough to become a game-changer. At the beginning of my purpose pursuit, there wasn't the title of 'Dr.' in front of my name. There was a constant battle in my mind about whether I was credentialed enough to lead a group of women. I didn't know if giving birth to my purpose was enough to qualify me for a leadership position. In my prayer time, the Holy Spirit reassured me that not only was I equipped, but I was even more equipped than some of those I admired. They had the degrees and credentials, but they relied more on their natural abilities than seeking their Creator for insight and revelation. The Holy Spirit assured me that He wasn't seeking the most eloquent speaker. He was looking for the willing heart that would seek Him for direction and guidance. He wanted a vessel that would obey Him and follow His direction. Because of my meekness and humility, He chose and qualified me.

While on your purpose journey, you will need to incorporate your faith as a guiding factor. Faith is the cornerstone of walking in your purpose. Faith requires us to put one foot in front of the other before seeing the complete manifestation. This is an area that many of us struggle with, as we want to control the outcome. For instance, if we are planning a conference, we need assurance that the tickets will sell before moving forward. Or, if we want to start a business, we want to know people will book and pay for our services before launching or investing our own money. If we want to write a book, we need a guarantee that it will be a bestseller before writing it. We want the satisfaction of the win before we endure the process. This, my friend, is not faith. You must believe the manifestation process will take place if you do your part as the steward. As long as you stay focused on the vision, you will reap the rewards that accompany discipline and diligence.

Over time, you will accept that you are a steward of your purpose. A steward is a keeper and not an owner. As a steward, our purpose is on loan to us. As a steward, our job is to take good care of what is entrusted to us without attempting to control or manipulate the final narrative. My prayer life shifted when I learned that I was the steward and not the owner. I am a firm believer that how you steward what you have been given determines how far you will go. Every day I consult the Owner (God) to get the direction for what has been entrusted to me and do the work without trying to figure out how it will end. After all, doesn't the manufacturer know what's best? This Kingdom mindset took away the fear, worry, doubt, and unnecessary pressure I had placed on my shoulder. This caused me to rest, understanding that the results of the outcome were not determined by me. My job as a steward included learning what I could to enhance and perfect my gifts, doing more purpose-filled work while spending constant, uninterrupted time doing less 'busy work,' and quietly building the 'ark.'

Protect Your Purpose

Just like how a mother protects a newborn baby, you will also need to protect your purpose. We protect our purpose by keeping it away from toxic environments and people. We protect our purpose by subscribing to platforms that bring life and nourishment to our souls. We protect our purpose by giving it back to God and seeking Him for direction. In the Bible, Hannah was a great example of this. She was barren for so many years and the constant center of ridicule. God heard her cries and blessed her womb with a son that she named Samuel. And in return, she kept her vow to God and gave her son back to Him. She gave up her son to serve in the temple with Eli the priest, and he later became a powerful prophet for the children of Israel, who had the distinction of anointing both Saul and David.

Could you have taken the bold step of faith and trust as Hannah did? Or would you try to keep the blessing for yourself? Isn't our release the true testament of our faith and trust in God? From my own experience, I can tell you that it is better to give God what belongs to him and watch Him bless and multiply the rest. The sacrifice of our gifts is no different than the sacrifice of our money. It all belongs to our Heavenly Father, and you must trust Him to be a promise keeper.

We also protect our purpose by keeping purpose blockers away from us- remember the list from the last chapter? A purpose blocker is anything that causes you to doubt or second-guess what you've been called to do. A purpose blocker can be a person, a job, or it can be any distraction that you allow to keep you from moving forward. You can also be your own purpose blocker when you have a defeatist mentality or if you have a spirit of self-sabotage. Any of these things can keep you from fulfilling your destiny.

Below is a list of some of the actions you can take to protect your purpose. Some of these will be daily activities, while others will be on a need-to basis. Feel free to add any personal revelations to this list.

Pray Over it Daily. Ask God to disclose and reveal anyone that does not have good intentions towards you. Before you make any moves, partner with anyone, or sign any deals, pray and ask God for direction. Everything will look good to you, especially when you first start. The enemy knows your weak spots, and he will send people to connect with you that seem like a perfect fit, but ultimately they have been sent to destroy you and assassinate your purpose. This is something that I have personally experienced more than once in my life. One incident was so detrimental and harmful that the effects could have destroyed my reputation and wiped out everything I had built. Always remember that prayer is your secret weapon.

> God gave these four young men an unusual aptitude for understanding every aspect of literature and wisdom. And God gave Daniel the special ability to interpret the meanings of visions and dreams. – Daniel 1:17 NLT

Never Stop Learning and Growing. Can you imagine the disservice that you would do as a parent by not educating your child? This is something you should also consider as it relates to fulfilling your purpose. There is always something new you can learn to keep your purpose moving and growing. Challenge yourself to learn everything you can to create an excellent product or service. Educating yourself in your purpose is learning all that you can in your area of focus. It does not necessarily mean that you need a college degree in a particular area, but you should consider getting the highest form of education that is available to you. Education comes in many forms – through God's word, commentaries, online courses, books, associations, mentorships, and coaching. Free education is available through blogs and online streaming. There is no excuse to not fully understand what is needed to operate in your purpose.

> So shall my word be that goeth forth out of my mouth: it shall not return unto me void, but it shall accomplish that which I please, and it shall prosper in the thing whereto I sent it. – Isaiah 55:11 KJV

Speak Life to It! Speaking the Word of God through scriptures and affirmations is critical to the health and growth of your purpose. Daily declarations and affirmations should be a part of your routine. The more you speak life, the more it will grow and flourish. Positive words produce positive outcomes. The opposite of this is true as well. If you are having a difficult time, which we all encounter from time to time, don't allow your negativity to seep in and change your confessions or taint your vision. Speak your words of affirmation out loud and put them in the atmosphere. Often when I am praying, I go outside and speak scriptures. When we come into agreement with God's Word, He promises that it will be accomplished. Ask the Holy Spirit to lead you to a particular scripture verse that you can apply to your purpose, and I encourage you to read and memorize it. Find the scripture that applies to your situation and stand on it.

> **Do not conform to the pattern of this world, but be transformed by the renewing of your mind. Then you will be able to test and approve what God's will is – his good, pleasing, and perfect will. – Romans 12:2**

Daily Renew Your Mind. Walking in your purpose is a work in progress. There will be days when you feel like going forward, and there will be days when you won't. Daily renewing your mind and thinking on good thoughts allows you to position yourself to see things the way that God sees them. The word 'renew' simply means to re-establish or repeat. During the process of renewing my mind, I erased the memories of the things that did not work in the past, and I focused on the opportunities that worked in my favor. Renewing requires you to look past your failures, the hurt, and the defeat. This is a training ground for the life of an overcomer. Once you learn to operate with a clear mind, you will know the difference between God talking to you and when you're the one who is speaking. Don't rehearse the failures. Learn from the failures but don't live in them.

> **But you are a chosen people, a royal priesthood, a holy nation, God's special possession, that you may declare the praises of him who called you out of darkness into his wonderful light. – 1 Peter 2:9 NIV**

Love and Embrace It! Count it as an honor and privilege to be called and chosen. Embrace the gift of discovering your purpose and all that you have been created to be. Accept the call, walk boldly in your assignment, stay focused, stay in your own lane, and don't compare your purpose to anyone else's. Comparison is the enemy of your purpose. You don't need to apologize for the anointing and favor on your life. Walk boldly in your call, doing the will of your Father.

> Surely He scorns the scornful, but gives grace to the humble. – Proverbs 3:34 NKJV

Stay Humble. Remaining humble is an essential key to successfully pursuing your purpose. God hates pride. Pride is more than just thinking you are better than someone else. Pride is a heart position that says you don't need God – you know what's best. There is a thin line between being proud or happy and being prideful. The prideful person says, "Oh, I know how to do that already." The humble person listens and then prays, "What is the right way to go?" Many people fail the pride test; they get off track once they receive recognition and accolades.

> You did not choose me, but I chose you and appointed you so that you might go and bear fruit—fruit that will last—and so that whatever you ask in my name the Father will give you. – John 15:16 NIV

Keep the Vision In Front of You. Remember what you were called to do by constantly reviewing your Purpose Vision Statement that you were encouraged to create in Chapter 6 of this book. Also, remember your 'why.' These constant reminders will help you stay motivated as you encounter challenges along the way.

> And David was greatly distressed; for the people spake of stoning him, because the soul of all the people was grieved, every man for his sons and for his daughters: but David encouraged himself in the Lord his God. – 1 Samuel 30:6 ESV

Celebrate Your Accomplishments. As you achieve various milestones, learn to celebrate them. Not only are you called to serve, but you are also called to live a fulfilling, rewarding, and prosperous life. Take time to celebrate your wins. I believe this is essential to you continuing on your journey. I can't express the number of times that I wanted to throw in the towel, feeling as if I was wasting my time and not seeing any tangible results. During these times, I looked back over the wins, the thank you notes, and the testimonies – and I was encouraged to continue.

> And the peace of God, which surpasses all understanding, will guard your hearts and minds through Christ Jesus. – Philippians 4:7 NIV

Detach When Necessary and Keep Your Peace. It's okay to take time for yourself. In my POWER Moms Volume I book, I spoke about the Supermom Syndrome and how it's good for us to remove the cape and connect to the essence of who we are. We need to do the things that bring us peace and serenity and allow ourselves some moments to breathe. Stay connected to the things that bring you peace.

> **Be anxious for nothing, but in everything by prayer and supplication, with thanksgiving, let your requests be made known to God. – Philippians 4:6 NKJV**

Pace Yourself. Be careful not to overwhelm yourself by having too much on your plate. Keep the Sabbath and rest as God did on the seventh day. Pay attention to what your body is telling you. Don't try to do too much at once. Set realistic goals, so you don't crash and burn.

> **Plans fail for lack of counsel, but with many advisers they succeed. – Proverbs 15:22 NIV**

Find Your Tribe. There will be parts of your journey where you will be required to walk alone, but there will be other times you will have to walk with others. Everyone must find their tribe. Your tribe includes your trusted advisors that are spiritually and naturally able to help guide you along. They may consist of family members, friends, or mentors. As you start to assemble your tribe, make sure that those giving you counsel are not self-appointed, but they have been appointed by God. Some well-meaning people can provide us with bad advice, so pray that the right people who are a part of your assignment will manifest on your journey. Also, keep in mind that some of your tribe members will be assigned for a season, and others will be assigned for a lifetime. Be open to the process as they may come and go. Guard your heart and move cautiously.

> Give thanks in all circumstances; for this is God's will for you in Christ Jesus. – 1 Thessalonians 5:18 NIV

Have an Attitude of Gratitude. In all things, give thanks. This has been one of my secret weapons. When things are spinning out of control, I focus on what's going right and thank God for those. I am even thankful for the things that go wrong because they often help me shift my perspective and learn how to do tasks more effectively and efficiently. They also spotlight the areas that I need to grow and mature in.

> Have I not commanded you? Be strong and courageous. Do not be afraid; do not be discouraged, for the Lord your God will be with you wherever you go. – Joshua 1:9 NIV

Silence Your Fears. It's almost inevitable that you will face fears and challenges as you pursue your purpose. These are the times that you will need to rely on your faith and trust more in the God that called you than in your natural abilities. Fears come with each level of success and accomplishment. Just be careful not to entertain it. Silence the voices by filling your thoughts with what God says about you. Create an atmosphere of praise and thanksgiving and focus on the vision.

Every day that you stay consistent and diligent, you open yourself to a new level. Accept the changes as they occur. Don't stunt your growth. Stay faithful in your purpose.

Are you ready to discover your purpose and live the life God has for you?

Join Dr. Sherrie on the journey at
www.manifestmypurpose.com

Chapter IX Recap

- God is looking for a willing heart that would seek Him for direction and guidance. He wants a vessel that will obey Him and follow His direction.

- Faith is the cornerstone of walking in your purpose.

- You are a steward of your purpose. A steward is a keeper and not an owner. As stewards, our purpose is on loan to us.

- We protect our purpose by keeping it away from toxic environments and people. We protect our purpose by subscribing to platforms that bring life and nourishment to our souls. We protect our purpose by giving it back to God and seeking Him for direction.

- A purpose blocker is anything that causes you to doubt or second-guess what you've been called to do.

- Remaining humble is an essential key to successfully pursuing your purpose.

Chapter X

LIVE YOUR PURPOSE-FULL LIFE

> *Now to Him who is able to do exceedingly abundantly above all that we ask or think, according to the power that works in us.* – Ephesians 3:20 KJV

WHEW! – ARE YOU still here? Go ahead and congratulate yourself. You stuck it out, and you should be proud! You have completed the hard work, and now it's time for you to step out into your new world full of purpose-filled opportunities. Just like a baby learning to walk, there will be wobbly legs and falls along the way. Don't let this stop you. You can do all things through Christ who strengthens you. Although the hard part has been done, you may still have hesitations and concerns about whether or not you're ready to walk the journey, or you may have some concerns about how to maneuver in this new space. This is perfectly okay as long as you keep moving ahead.

The POWER Moms© is my network of amazing women that I've enjoyed working with on a series of books, workshops, and conferences entitled 'The POWER Moms Series.' The acronym POWER stands for Persevere, Overcome, Win, Empower, and Restore. I love this anthology because I had the privilege of partnering with many first-time authors – women who knew they had a story but did not have an open platform to share it. I interviewed and carefully selected each potential author by asking them a series of questions to better help me understand if their story and message were a fit for the audience our books reach. Generally, all of our conversations started with me asking them to tell me their story. I am always amazed at how women with some of the most challenging backgrounds have found a way to tap into who they are. Often, without them even knowing it, they have discovered their purpose. I love hearing them come alive when they take the bold step of telling where they have been and where they are going. They motivate me to keep growing in my purpose.

But let's just say for the sake of this book that these women retreated when they experienced physical abuse, abandonment, failure, rejection, divorce, and the list of negative experiences goes on and on. What if they would have stopped? I believe that if they had remained silent, they would have been disobedient and could have possibly forfeited their promise. The Bible states that God's gifts come without repentance; although the gift is yours, if you never claim it, you will never receive it. If you never allow your story to pass from victim to victor, you will stay stuck and defeated. The Bible also tells us in Revelations 9:11, *"And they overcame him by the blood of the Lamb, and by the word of their testimony."* Your testimony is your public acknowledgment. As you are learning more about yourself and your purpose, I want to encourage you to use your testimony as an opportunity to help others. You don't need a ministry platform to bring a word of encouragement or help shape someone's destiny.

When I work with my client authors, I encourage them to tell their stories through the pages of their book. It doesn't matter what type of book they are writing – there is an opportunity for them to connect to their audience by sharing a personal story from their life, one where they have learned a valuable lesson. As you move forward and move out, think about how your story, whether written or not, can bring light to someone else's path. This is how you live a purposeful life.

Become Unstoppable

It's time for you to impact others with your purpose. Your days of blending in the background and solely cheering for others that fearlessly pursue their purpose are over. It's time to quit playing the blame game. The truth is, whatever you have faced doesn't disqualify you from doing whatever you need to do to pursue your purpose. It's time for you to pull it together and live a purposeful life. You've reached a place in your purpose journey where it's time for you to start allowing your baby to walk independently. You have the tools you need to stretch your faith and walk. The only person or thing that can stop you from flowing in your purpose is you, not the lack of money, support, friends, or even the roof caving in. Satan himself can't stop the plan of God from manifesting in your life. You have the power to proceed with purpose. I believe that as you have read this book, there is a determination that has risen on the inside of you that will give you the tenacity and endurance you need to fulfill your purpose. I have emphasized this a few times throughout this book – there will be times that you will get discouraged, or you'll question if it's really worth it. The enemy's job is to constantly tell you that you are not equipped for the job, and you already know that's not true. God is a God of completion. He finishes what He starts.

> **And I am convinced and sure of this very thing, that He Who began a good work in you will continue until the day of Jesus Christ [right up to the time of His return], developing [that good work] and perfecting and bringing it to full completion in you. – Philippians 1:6 Amplified**

I wish I'd had this knowledge earlier in my journey. When it was time for me to step into my purpose, I remember the words "dream bigger" being etched in my mind. I wasn't much of a dreamer. Although I said I had faith, I was the practical girl that found myself trusting more in my ability and things that I could physically see. I had been so discouraged by life that I just stopped dreaming. I don't know when that day actually occurred, but I remember how it affected my life. Instead of pushing my faith and speaking God's word, I dealt with life as it was handed to me. I was often so caught up in what was in front of me, I did not allow myself much hope for the future. That's called self-sabotage. Don't allow self-sabotage to be your friend. Trust me, I used to know her, and she's not loyal. She will throw you under the bus with any opportunity she gets. She's the type that always wants a ride but never has any gas money. She's the type that goes out to eat with you but conveniently leaves her wallet at home. She's a user, and once she's done with you, she'll move on to another hopeful God-fearing woman and crush her dreams as well. Self-sabotage appears in many different characteristics like procrastination, excuses, laziness, and fears. You'll need to pay attention to this.

    I had a conversation with one of my mentees about her fear of leaving her job because she felt she needed the money. At the time, she knew she was being stretched, pushed, and redirected to pursue her purpose but was afraid that she wouldn't be able to make enough money to pay her bills if she left her job. I recognized that fear. I used to think money equaled security. Over time, God taught me that He was my source and that He would make provision for the vision entrusted to me. In other words, I didn't need anyone to finance my dreams if I learned to rely solely on Him; He would direct me to the right connections to ensure my needs were met. Let me reiterate, I am not talking about working a job instead of working a full-time business. Although

I advocate for you having multiple streams of revenue, I believe that you'll be led to finding the best avenue that is the right fit for you.

Be Fruitful and Multiply

> For whoever has, to him more will be given, and he will have abundance; but whoever does not have, even what he has will be taken away from him. – Matthew 13:12

After making a commitment to pursuing my purpose, my gifts started to be revealed to me. Things that I did easily and effortlessly, I noticed that others didn't do them as easily or as efficiently. My gift of writing was one of those gifts. Once I realized this, God gave me the wisdom to create a consistent stream that I could multiply. Today I teach women multiple ways to monetize their gifts, even if they have only one gift. It is my understanding that these gifts that God has entrusted to you will be used to create a steady flow of income into your hands. This is the Kingdom multiplication principle©. When you couple your gifts with your giving to God's Kingdom (tithing), He becomes involved in helping you monetize it. Let me explain a little further. My gift is writing, and with this one gift, I can produce additional streams of revenue, including:

- Writing books and selling them.
- Creating digital courses relating to the subjects in my books.

- Teaching others how to write their books.
- Helping others publish their books.
- Selling online courses about book writing.
- Selling online courses about book publishing.
- Offering to ghostwrite for those that want to write books but aren't good at writing or have the time.

Do you see how this works? One gift has been segmented into a business that creates multiple streams. I can guarantee that there is always a steady stream of income coming in because this one gift alone has turned into numerous opportunities. In addition to my writing, I also book speaking engagements and secure business coaching clients, and with those, there are nine different streams of income coming into my business. I don't want to oversimplify it because it was not an overnight process. What I want you to grasp is, once I started making God a priority in my finances – giving ten percent from all sources of income, the Holy Spirit helped me organize and package my gifts in a way that produced wealth.

Do you recall the 'Parable of the Talents' that I referenced at the opening of this book? Take some time to become familiar with that scripture and meditate on it. My biggest takeaway from the story is if you bury your gift or just keep it for yourself without allowing it an opportunity to increase and multiply, you are doing yourself and God a disservice. Don't be like that servant who buried his talent – be found faithful when your Master returns to see what you have created from the seeds (purpose) you have been given. If you are a person that likes to give everything away, start with the 10% rule. Donate 10% of your time, talent, and treasure to your church or an organization you volunteer for. The Bible tells us that our gifts will make room for us and bring us before great men. Don't feel guilty about using your gifts to create revenue and profits. As you move forward in your purpose, find ways to generate income with the gifts you have. There are a million ways to use your seed traits to create the life you envision.

Give Your Purpose Direction

Ultimately when you are a believer, you must know that monetizing your gifts is about creating revenue to help build God's Kingdom and serving others. If this is not your belief, let me say it another way. Your money is more about you bringing good into this world and helping others, not just about how lavish of a lifestyle you can live. I used to confess that I was a millionaire. After about a year of saying this, one day, the Holy Spirit asked me, "If you were a millionaire, what would you do with it?" When I started rambling off all of the things I would buy for myself and my family, He said it another way. "If you had a million dollars **right now**, what would you do with it?" At that moment, I had to be honest and admit that I wanted to be rich for my own pursuit and gain. Being a millionaire was a personal goal with selfish intentions. That day, I decided to help as many people as I could become free in their minds and released from spiritual bondage. The finances that come into my hands are planted first in my local church, our ministry, my family's needs, and then we help others in need by giving to missions. This has translated into my family being able to walk out the scripture in Proverbs 19:17 ESV "whoever is generous to the poor lends to the Lord, and He will repay him for his deed. Now that I have tapped into God's way of living, I see the tangible evidence of His provision and overflow that my family and I now enjoy. Living a purposeful life means submitting your finances to God and allowing Him to be in control. It's His money anyway. He's just looking for good stewards.

> "When you ask, you do not receive, because you ask with wrong motives, that you may spend what you get on your pleasures." – James 4:3 NIV

If you ever wonder why people who don't serve God sometimes seem wealthier than people who do, I can guarantee that they are operating off the principle of sowing and reaping. They are working diligently in their purpose and being intentional about how they live their life. They may not be sowing money to a ministry, but I can almost guarantee you that they support a cause they believe in. I always say that God's principles and laws work no matter who is using them. There are laws to living and fully operating in your gifts and benefitting from the profits resulting from the alignment of the principle.

> "Give, and it will be given to you: good measure, pressed down, shaken together, and running over will be put into your bosom. For with the same measure that you use, it will be measured back to you." – Luke 6:38

I referenced my moving to Texas quite a bit throughout this book because it was that move that catapulted me to my destiny. It was letting go of one thing and trusting and believing that there was more to me and my family's story. Our story of relocating resembled the children of Israel's journey to their promised land. The Red Sea parted on many occasions for us, and things that would have been a 'no' according to man's standards became a 'yes' according to God's standards. Opportunities for business and financial increase became available without following the standard rules of having a website or a working phone. My husband and I still discuss how customers would reach out via email, and I would have to call them back from the hotel phone. Despite the uncertainty of life, there was one thing that I held on to, and that was the words and promises found in Psalms 23.

While writing my first book, I sat in Barnes and Noble and cried out to God. The tears became so heavy that I went into the bathroom so no one would see me. I attempted to pull myself together, but the tears just wouldn't stop coming down my face. I walked out of the stall and looked in the mirror, and I became angry with God and asked Him, "Why did you lead us here? Where are you?" Immediately, the words of Psalms 23 rolled off my tongue as more tears streamed down my face. I recited the Psalm until the tears stopped. Looking back, I know it was God's way of telling me that He did not leave us and that He was making a way for us.

Outside of the joys of pursuing purpose, there will be those moments when you ask, "God are you there?" These are the moments when He reassures us that He will never leave us. Walking in your purpose will be the most rewarding experience you will ever encounter. It will produce joy and fulfillment. You will feel like you've been reborn. I want to encourage you today to be the person you see in your dreams. Move on from the things that once were and walk in the newness of life. Enjoy this new spiritual motherhood – your purpose will develop, mature, and blossom into greatness. Remember you are the steward, be found worthy of your call. You can create whatever you need. Use the Word of God as your reference.

This has been a fantastic journey we have taken together. I am so honored that you trusted me enough to read through and soak up the wisdom in these pages. I poured out everything I had on these pages, opening up my personal stories to let you know that you are not alone. Purpose has been calling you for quite some time, and now is your time to go forward. Each time we are faced with a new chapter in our lives, the enemy of our souls will want us to believe that we are not good enough, we are not worthy enough, or we are not prepared. I can almost envision the warfare that takes place in Heaven when we as believers decide we want to pursue God's perfect will and plan for our life. I always notice when I am on track for something significant and groundbreaking because all hell breaks loose – do you notice that too? Go back through this book and review the things that were revealed to you. I desire that this is the beginning of the best years of your life. As we close this book, I release this prayer and decree over you.

You have been positioned for this time and season, and it's time for you to take flight and soar. I rebuke every spirit that will try to hinder or derail you, including doubt, nervousness, procrastination, laziness, stubbornness, anxiousness, comparison, unbelief, and low self-esteem. I decree and declare you will walk in boldness and authority and become the total woman God has called you to be – mind, body, soul, and spirit. I speak life and growth to your purpose. I loose the spirit of creativity, ingenious, a sound mind, focus, completion, wisdom, and self-worth over you, in Jesus' name!

Go forth and conquer all.
Blessings to you.

PURPOSE NOTES:

_____
_____
_____
_____
_____
_____
_____
_____
_____
_____
_____
_____
_____
_____
_____
_____

ACKNOWLEDGMENTS:

My Family:

Pastors Darrell & Vivian Roberts (my mom and dad)

My Former Youth Pastor – Alonzo Denson *(Rest in Heaven)*

The POWER Moms© and my circle of supporters

Apostle Brenda Cole
Yvette Phillips
Cacilie Hughes-Gaston

ABOUT THE AUTHOR:

HER EXCELLENCY, DR. SHERRIE Walton, is a United Nations Ambassador at Large, Guest Lecturer, Keynote Speaker, Author, Global Entrepreneur, University Lecturer, Film Producer, Publisher, Spiritual and Life Coach and "Mompreneur" Mogul.

She travels around the world empowering, connecting, and restoring women's lives, helping them unlock their voice and discover their purpose. Her mission is to impact the lives of over One Million women, reaching one woman at a time. Her empowering words of wisdom bring her audiences to standing ovations as she encourages them to live their best fearless life right now. Dr. Sherrie has overcome many of life's adversities and is building a platform for other Mompreneurs to pursue their dreams, no matter what their past is. She is an advocate for women building other strong women and believes that life truly has no limits.

Dr. Sherrie entered the world of Entrepreneurship over 18 years ago. After becoming the youngest black Insurance Broker in three years at a Fortune 500 company, she exited corporate America to become a full-time entrepreneur. In

2002, Dr. Sherrie co-founded her first event company and went on to service celebrity clientele, earning her first feature in 'Style Me Pretty Florida' and Essence online magazines.

Dr. Sherrie is the founder of Sherrie Walton Consulting and co-founder of Walton Publishing House. She helps authors birth their "book dreams" and creates compilation books and platforms for women speakers, business owners, and everyday people. Dr. Sherrie is the founder and creator of the 'Mommy & Me Dream Bigger Tour,' an international multi-city (2) day experience that teaches moms and kids how to overcome their fears, pursue their dreams and reshape their lives. 'Kidz Biz in the Box' is a spin-off business venture led by Dr. Sherrie and her 3 children, which helps Kidpreneuers start and grow their businesses.

Dr. Sherrie has received Congressional Recognition for her contributions to the City of Houston. She has also received recognition from the Mayor of Houston, honoring Women Making a Difference, Houston's 40 Under 40 Next Generation of Leaders Award, and recognized as an Emerging Business for the Miami Superbowl. She has partnered with major brands to host events, including Neiman Marcus, Bloomingdales, Eden Roc Miami, and a host of other luxury companies. As the creator of 'POWER Moms,' she received a proclamation in Waco, Texas, naming March 9th as 'POWER Moms Day.' She is the Daniel and Esther Global Network CEO and the Vice President of Operations for both the Wisdom International Ministerial Alliance (WIMA) and Greatness Publishing companies.

Dr. Sherrie is a Licensed Minister, the co-founder of Wildfire Ministries, and she partners with her husband as a Spiritual and Life Coach to NBA Players with Family First Sports Firm. In addition, she is a Marriage Coach and has been married to Dr. Christopher Walton for 18+ years. Together they have three beautiful children, Chris II, age 13; Kai-Milan, age 10; and Winter, age 8.

Dr. Sherrie has been seen on ABC News, Fox News, CEO Mom, and various media outlets.

CONNECT WITH ME!

It will encourage me to hear from you. It's like a woman that gives birth to a baby. Although the mommy believes her baby is beautiful, she loves to listen to onlookers' compliments, so let me know how you think my "baby" looks.

If there is anything in this book that resonates with your spirit, please email me: admin@iamsherriewalton.com or leave me a message on my website at: www.iamsherriewalton.com.

Website: www.iamsherriewalton.com

Social media:
Linked In: www.linkedin.com/in/drsherrie
Instagram: www.instagram.com/drsherriewalton
Facebook: www.facebook.com/IamSherrieWalton

Coaching inquires: admin@iamsherriewalton.com

For bookings, email: admin@iamsherriewalton.com
For products visit: www.iamsherriewalton.com

Other books by the author, published by Walton Publishing House / www.waltonpublishinghouse.com

40 Day Devotional for the Savvy Mompreneur
God, Fix My Marriage
POWER Moms – Volumes I & II
POWER Moms 3.0
Write it! Tap into your POWER and write your best-selling books in 90 days

Books available at www.iamsherriewalton.com
Amazon
Barnes and Nobles
Target
Books A Million
and wherever books are sold.

www.ingramcontent.com/pod-product-compliance
Lightning Source LLC
Chambersburg PA
CBHW071417070526
44578CB00003B/587